POLITICS

AND AMBIGUITY

RHETORIC OF THE HUMAN SCIENCES

Lying Down Together: Law, Metaphor, and Theology
Milner S. Ball

Politics and Ambiguity
William E. Connolly

The Rhetoric of Economics
Donald N. McCloskey

Therapeutic Discourse and Socratic Dialogue
Tullio Maranhão

Heracles' Bow: Essays on the Rhetoric and Poetics of the Law
James Boyd White

Politics
and Ambiguity

WILLIAM E. CONNOLLY

THE UNIVERSITY OF WISCONSIN PRESS

Published 1987

The University of Wisconsin Press
114 North Murray Street
Madison, Wisconsin 53715

The University of Wisconsin Press, Ltd.
1 Gower Street
London WC1E 6HA, England

Copyright © 1987
The Board of Regents of the University of Wisconsin System
All rights reserved

First printing

Printed in the United States of America

For LC CIP information see the colophon

ISBN 0-299-10990-9

CONTENTS

PREFACE

Is it possible to cast off teleological assumptions accepted by contemporary defenders of civic virtue and the common good while still defending a set of social and political virtues? To believe in the indispensability of a common good while insisting that even the highest historical achievements are incorrigibly ambiguous in character? To criticize contemporary theories of the self as subject (or agent) while endorsing the subject as an essentially ambiguous achievement of modernity? To adopt ingredients from a genealogical mode of critique while offering morally toned interpretations of the contemporary political economy? These essays are presented in the conviction that such a dual orientation is internally defensible, and, moreover, that the interwoven character of freedom, politics, and ambiguity emerges most luminously when thought is nourished by such a perspective. They seek both to defend a political theory in the early stages of its development by displaying its ability to identify sore spots in those orientations now competing for hegemony in public discourse and to accent distinctive elements in the contemporary political economy circumscribed by established theories.

I do not hope to still every doubt about this project in the course of these few essays. Some of the doubts persist as moments in my own thinking. But the essay format does provide an appropriate medium for presenting these ideas in their current state of development. That format provides opportunities to play out and play with the perspective, to multiply occasions in which apparently disparate elements are brought to bear on each other in ways that might loosen the hold established political debates exercise over us. That, anyway, is the hope that encourages me to gather these essays together.

From the vantage point of the perspective to be advanced, we inhabit an order that simultaneously extends disciplinary pressures into new corners of the common life and insinuates them more insistently into the interior of the self. That is not to say that everyone interiorizes these disciplines in the same way; nonetheless, each self and the character of the common life are profoundly affected by these developments. Some constituencies interiorize them; others resist or subvert the disciplines they resent and thus place themselves in jeopardy of receiving new ones; others yet react with persistent ambivalence, striving to evade them personally while insisting fervently upon their strict applicability to other constituencies.

The first task is to identify the character of these disciplinary pressures; the second is to chart the heterogeneous responses to them and the cumulative implications of these responses for the health of the order; the third is to identify their sources; and the fourth is to ascertain how they might be relieved in ways that enhance prospects for freedom under the circumstances of contemporary life. If I exaggerate the prominence of these disciplines from time to time, that should not be too surprising. For the point is to discern future possibilities residing in these actualities by locating their trajectory and the logic that propels them.

The above assertions about the self, discipline, and the order are inherently controversial. It is not simply that people will disagree about the extent to which new incentive systems, bureaucratic regulations, modes of surveillance, and especially (as I shall call them) "unconscious contrivances of social control" have been consolidated. A more legitimate matter of controversy is how these contrivances are to be interpreted in their relation to the self and the order. Are they in part a political response to the disaffection many manifest from the roles assigned to them? And does this disaffection itself reflect a sense that the future which contemporary institutions are designed to build now seems both more perilous and less credible to newly recruited role bearers? Is it, further, that while many disciplines are presented as means to improve or fulfill or enable the self, some actually help to constitute failures, needs, and disabilities to which they respond? Are they responses to the needs of the self or formations that spawn more needy selves?

They are doubtless all these things and others besides. But to say, as I do, that we experience today an amplification of "disciplinary pressures" is to interpret the increase in mechanisms of coordination, evaluation, and control as a sign of cracks and fissures in the good life we share; it is also to contest alternative interpretations that treat the increase as a more efficient means to a good life still secure in its structure. If each new element of discipline is light in itself, the composite package is unbearably light in weight. For these impositions reveal too much about the future they portend, and they reduce the weight of tacit identification with that future. This process of collective unburdening disorients participants and magnifies the dialectic of role disaffection and disciplinary response plaguing the order.

Though the character and epistemic status of this claim will be presented in the main body of the text, perhaps one central issue to be joined can be introduced more concretely through an example. The "Science Times" section of *The New York Times* periodically summarizes psychological research into newly discovered pathologies or "syndromes" revolving around sexual life, body weight, personal dependability, humor, intelligence, and aggression. The structure of these summaries is typified by a recent report entitled "Deep-Seated Causes for Procrastination."[1] Here a new neurosis called the "procrastination syndrome" is revealed, and its causes are traced to the character of those afflicted by it. Procrastinators are people with deep "internal conflicts." Some delay because they "fear failure and negative evaluation"; others because they unconsciously "resist control" by superiors. There are other causes of this syndrome poorly understood at the moment: more research into its sources and the appropriate corrective therapy is needed.

The research presupposes those assumptions most in need of interrogation. It assumes that the most salient source of the syndrome is to be found deep within the self, that these internal causes reflect conflicts which inhibit the self from realizing its own potentialities most fully, and that tactics devised to relieve the phenomenon bear no notable relation to the politics of disciplinary control. The model of individual and social integration governing the research is not itself subjected to interrogation. It never occurs to the researchers that the extension of performance norms into new areas of life might produce the deviations they trace to "deep" internal conflicts. Nor does it ever occur to them to question just why this mysterious metaphor "deep" attaches itself so securely to discourse into the internal psychology of the self and so precariously to those social rules and structures that help to constitute the interior of the contemporary self.

While the example is trivial enough, the possibility of its endless replication carries untrivial political implications. For that which from one perspective constitutes a discovery of internal conflicts in a self otherwise amenable to internal integration constitutes from another the insertion of disciplinary pressures into a self that enhance its vulnerability to normalizing control. What further presents itself in the first perspective as a standard of normality responsive to the self's pursuit of self-integration appears in the second as the imposition of norms upon a self not disposed in itself to this politics of normalization.

If there are alternative possibilities of interpretation here, why does contemporary discourse so readily locate "procrastination" in the anti-

1. *New York Times*, April 12, 1983.

punctual self rather than in an institutional structure that imposes the norm of punctuality upon resistant selves? What are the cumulative political effects of the operational assumption that the self becomes fulfilled as internal impediments to its integration within established ends of the order are removed? What, more fundamentally, is the philosophical status of the idea that one must be an integrated individual to be a secure bearer of rights and interests? Or, for that matter, what is the status of the ghostly counterideal of the virtuous self which realizes itself through integrative participation in the life of a rational community? And how would the politics of individual and social integration appear if we suspended both ideals of self simultaneously (instead of insisting upon criticizing either only from the assured conviction that the other can be sustained)?

I pose these issues as questions because the responses given in this text do not correspond to either antinomy presented above and because they are presented as a series of thought experiments. The idea is not to disprove the controlling assumptions in the theories opposed, for they were not susceptible to proof in the first place. The idea is to proceed on the basis of alternative assumptions to ascertain, first, how the world is then experienced, and, second, how the new experience engendered by this disturbance lifts the aura of necessity or self-evidence surrounding the established terms of debate. That, at any rate, is the most promising way to free thought from the grooves already prepared for it and to inject alternative possibilities of experience into life.

Chapter 1, entitled "Democracy and Normalization," introduces several themes to be elaborated in later chapters. It calls for a shift in the "social ontology" that governs discourse about democratic politics. It suggests, first, that distinctive virtues of democratic politics are appreciated best if the democratic ideal is articulated within the frame of an ontology of "dissonant holism," and second, that political efforts to subdue normalizing tendencies within democratic political economies will be given greater legitimacy from the vantage point of that same framework.

The next several essays seek to delineate some of the disciplines that have crystallized in recent years, to show how the quest for personal identity and the structural imperatives of the political economy collide to foster a politics of resentment and disaffection, and to call into question the relation between the identity citizens seek to fulfill and the future the political economy is designed to realize. They seek to encourage radicalism and liberalism in their opposition to intrusions from the right while trying to understand how the politics of both have helped to generate the reactions they decry. This discussion is developed through critiques of interpretations offered by Samuel Huntington, George Gilder, Michael Walzer, Jürgen Habermas, and Michel Foucault.

Chapter 6, entitled "The Dilemma of Legitimacy," draws these scattered contentions together and then explores alterations in the ideal of legitimacy that might be suggested by this account. Those latter suggestions are elaborated in the next few essays through an examination of Foucault's theory of self, discipline, and order, through a critique of the recent work of Richard Rorty, and through a discussion of the ambiguous orientation to authority appropriate to this perspective. The controlling contention here is that the competing ideals of individualism and communalism, liberalism and radicalism, negative freedom and positive freedom, tend to converge in obscuring the ambiguous character of standards, ideals, and ends most worthy of endorsement. To rectify this depreciation of ambiguity is to improve the case for introducing greater porosity or "slack" into the institutional order and, thereby, to encourage a democratic polity to give more space to the otherness generated by its own ideals and necessities. The guiding intuition here was articulated by Simone de Beauvoir in an early work: "As long as there have been men and they lived, they have all felt this tragic ambiguity of their condition, but as long as there have been philosophers and they have thought, most of them have tried to mask it."[2] Beauvoir is on the mark in her first assertion. But philosophers do not monopolize the urge to mask ambiguities in those standards and practices closely interwoven with the identities we seek to sustain. It is operative in each of us. And it encompasses more than a psychological disposition: it incorporates epistemic and moral dimensions within its fold, and the failure to contest it in all its complexity carries significant implications for the character of disciplinary politics. Finally, the case for appreciating ambiguities lodged in modern ideals of self, politics, and social life is to be made not only at the level of the individual experience (as the de Beauvoir assertion may suggest); these ambiguities must be given institutional expression as well. Only in this way can the "other" in the self and the order—that which is first produced and then debased by established conventions—be given its due. This is the field upon which the politics of freedom and unfreedom is waged confidentially today.

The last chapter, "Where the Word Breaks Off," continues this account and clarifies the peculiar relation of these themes to the knowledge enterprise. For while knowing is definitely essential to political

---

2. *The Ethics of Ambiguity,* trans. Bernard Frechtman (Secaucus: Citadel Press, 1972), p. 7.

thought, it does not exhaust it; it is also necessary to think genealogically about ways in which the will to knowledge can suppress ambiguity in life. The relation of social life to its linguistic modes of expression provides the medium through which this clarification is offered. After endorsing available critiques of the "designative" and "constitutive" theories, two perspectives are examined which converge in opposing this first pair but diverge in other respects. I have labeled them the expressive and the genealogical theories, treating Charles Taylor as a preeminent spokesman for the first and Friedrich Nietzsche and Michel Foucault as the most effective representatives of the second. I adopt a qualified version of the second theory. That position enables the self to distance itself from some of the norms applied to it; and it immunizes the perspective from the various charges of self-refutation or self-contradiction commonly brought in America against theories of this type. It also poses intriguing questions about the epistemic status of those theories that recurrently compete for hegemony in the contemporary setting.

Critical thought, because of the breadth of issues it must encompass and the relative dearth of secure guideposts, is typically fragmented by comparison to the more settled conventions it seeks to disrupt. These essays, I am afraid, provide no exception to this rule. I sometimes find myself wandering off into unfamiliar territory, and, especially in the later essays, it is occasionally unclear to me whether I am advancing a thesis, pursuing a thought, or reiterating a slogan with implications still to be unraveled. Since these are thoughts on the way, I have not always resolved this ambivalence.

My relation to my own thought is of intense interest merely to me. Might it also be that the contemporary condition calls for thinking that suspends a few settled assumptions and shakes down debates contained within that space of reassurance?

ACKNOWLEDGMENTS

I am greatly indebted to Jane Bennett, Thomas Dumm, Jean Elshtain, Richard Flathman, Alex Hooke, Mike Shapiro, and Mort Schoolman for criticisms of earlier drafts of these essays. I would also like to acknowledge participants in the NEH faculty seminar at the University of Massachusetts in the summer of 1984 whose friendly and skeptical engagement with these arguments helped me to develop them further. I owe a peculiar debt to George Kateb, Charles Taylor, and Sheldon Wolin. The voice of each has become part of an interior conversation within me; each jostles for space, and none (in my soul) is quite contented with the room available to it.

Finally, though I did not know Michel Foucault, these essays wrestle with dimensions of his thought. They seek to appreciate the distinctive power of his perspective without politicizing life so relentlessly that an indispensable dimension of politics disappears from view.

Chapters one, nine and ten are published here for the first time. The others, though some appear here in revised form, have been published previously. Thanks are due to the following publishers for permission to publish these essays in this text.

"The Politics of Reindustrialization," *Democracy* (July 1981): 9–22.

"The Democratic Party and Civic Disaffection," *Democracy* (July 1982): 18–28.

"Progress, Growth and Pessimism in America," *Democracy* (October 1983): 15–30.

"The Critical Theory of Jürgen Habermas," *History and Theory* (October 1979): 397–418, Copyright © 1979, by Wesleyan University.

"The Dilemma of Legitimacy," *What Should Political Theory Be Now?*, edited by John Nelson (Albany: State University of New York Press 1983), 337–82.

"Discipline, Politics and Ambiguity," *Political Theory* (August 1983): 325–41.

"The Mirror of America," *Raritan* (Summer 1983): 124–34.

"Modern Authority and Ambiguity," forthcoming in *Authority Revisited: Nomos XXIX*, edited by John Chapman and Roland Pennock (New York: New York University Press). Copyright © 1986 by New York University and by permission of New York University Press.

POLITICS

AND AMBIGUITY

1

DEMOCRACY

AND NORMALIZATION

The Ambiguity of Democracy

Democracy is the pride and the hope of modernity. It also contains danger. The danger does not flow merely from forces hostile to democratic institutions. It resides within the ideal itself.

Democracy makes the state accountable to the people; it reduces unwarranted privilege; it protects the rights of citizens; it fosters allegiance to the public good by implicating its members in common projects; it encourages a healthy skepticism toward rules, authority, laws, experts, and regulations; it enables skeptical citizens to curtail governmental officials bent upon a destructive course.

Other types of state do some of these things to some degree. But democracy combines them and balances the oppositions among them in distinctive ways. For, when it functions in accord with its essential purpose, a democracy treats its members as citizens; more significantly, it fosters institutions and traditions that encourage individuals to expect this treatment as a matter of course. Periodic elections, due process, constitutional protection of basic rights, the publication of laws and policies, public dialogue over the wisdom of alternative programs and candidates—these practices infuse respect for persons into the public realm. And people treated with respect and dignity in one realm of life are, first, more likely to insist upon respect in other areas, and, second, better equipped to wrest that dignity from people and institutions reluctant to bestow it.[1] Democratic institutions foster a robust, skeptical citizenry who give allegiance to the order partly because it nourishes these qualities in them; and the citizens in turn provide the institutions with the creative energies essential to a vibrant public life.

---

1. The ways in which citizenship helps to foster individuality are nicely developed by George Kateb, in "The Moral Distinctiveness of Representative Democracy" (*Ethics* [April 1981]). My disagreement with Kateb revolves around his depreciation of normalizing tendencies built into the ideal of democracy and into the structure of the American political economy. A thoughtful critique/appreciation of Kateb's essay is developed by Morton Schoolman in "Liberalism's Ambiguous Legacy: Individuality and Technological Constraints" (*Research in Philosophy and Technology* 7 [1984]:229–54).

Democracy and Normalization

The democratic citizen, I am suggesting, is less willing than members of other societies to be a mere stone in an edifice. The democratic citizen is more likely to weigh fateful public decisions to ascertain their effects on the common good today or tomorrow. He or she is more likely to dissent from or protest or resist or organize to overturn arbitrary treatment and policies. The unwillingness to be a stone in an edifice contributes over the long term to the health of democratic society. That, anyway, is the faith that makes democracy the pride and hope of modernity.

There is a large gap between this idealization and the actual practice of democratic states. We notice the gap because we are pulled by the ideal. Or, better, we define the difference as a discrepancy when we are pulled by that dimension of democracy idealized here.

For if citizens are unsuited to serve merely as role bearers in a large enterprise, an opposing element in the democratic ideal nonetheless functions to grind them into material for use. The hope and the danger reside inside the same ideal; they are not neatly separable into two competing "conceptions of democracy."

Perhaps the briefest way to discern this connection is to recall that Rousseau, seeking freedom for all citizens, found it necessary to implicate each morally in the laws governing all. Only in this way, he thought, could laws be experienced not as impediments to one's freedom but as expressions of one's citizenship. This idea continues to have an important presence in modern understandings of citizenship, freedom, and democracy. And once Rousseau's strictures against size, commercialism, gender equality, and foreign involvement have been lifted, the area of life covered by regulations in which the citizen is to be implicated can be seen to expand magnificently.

The best-known interpretations of Rousseau emphasize the connection between his ideal of communal freedom and his insistence that the individual identify with the standards of the polity. This emphasis, congenial to individualists who seek to differentiate their views of freedom and democracy from Rousseauian theory, is not false; but it does ignore a feature of Rousseau's thought shared with his modern critics: his recognition that the customs and norms constituting a way of life are not natural but artificial, not discovered but formed conventions. "But the social order is a sacred right," Rousseau says, "that serves as a basis for all others. However that right does not come from nature; it is therefore based on conventions."[2]

2. *On the Social Contract*, ed. Roger Masters, trans. Judith Masters (New York: St. Martin's Press, 1978), p. 47.

If a form of life is known by its participants to be conventional, then established traditions will be experienced as hateful restraints unless they are submitted to the will either of the individual or the collectivity. Enhancement of the willful and conventional character of life—an enhancement that helps to define the character of modernity itself—can thereby also deepen the experience of unfreedom among participants. Modern democracy seeks to make life more free, more the result of willed convention than tradition unreflectively followed or behavior disconnected from will. It thus draws a larger portion of life into the fold of thematized norms. And by thereby enlarging the field of potential conduct deemed to be abnormal, it exerts internal pressure on participants to identify with established norms in order to establish themselves as free agents. In this setting one is unfree to the extent that (a) one is governed by traditions unthematized publicly; (b) one is governed by conventions undemocratically established; (c) one is governed by democratically established conventions at odds with one's will; (d) one falls below the threshold of normality needed to qualify as an agent capable of free or autonomous conduct. The close relation between modernity and the experience of alienation is bound up with this more fundamental set of connections among the conventionalization of life, democratization, free agency, and the enlargement of the sphere of commonality.

Democratic theory and practice thus contain an ambiguous space in which individuality and commonality are simultaneously differentiated and pressed to harmonize more closely. The periodic drive to expand the scope of democratic participation can be seen as an attempt to resolve this ambiguity with respect to norms recently drawn into the sphere of thematized conventions. The conversion of traditions governing gender relations, sexuality, education, child rearing, and work into contestable conventions encourages the effort to foster identification with them through participation in their creation. The ambiguity is to be dissolved either by changing the will of participants to foster identification or by changing the conventions to conform to the will. But the ways in which structural limits inhibit the restructuring of conventions tend to skew the process toward the first pole of this continuum. And participation seldom seems to bring the dividends it promises for freedom: one constellation of hostile and resentful citizens is spawned by that action which temporarily satisfies the other's sense of justice in the established order of things. The tenacity of the ambiguity is underplayed by those who believe that participation is its solution.

Democratic theorists also tend to try to dissolve an issue that is inherently indissoluble, and these attempts blind them to one set or another

Democracy and Normalization

of the normalizing pressures inherent in democracy. The individualist seeks resolution by stating formal conditions for individual agency while hesitating to acknowledge the drive within democracy itself to close the gap between the identity of the self as a free agent and the social roles and norms with which the self is to identify. Any normalizing pressures observed are then projected onto features of modern life alien to democracy. Advocates of the politics of the common good obscure the ambiguity by insisting that, when properly institutionalized, individuality and commonality harmonize nicely. The individual is to be "situated" within a common good which realizes the essential good in the self.[3]

The debate between individualists and communalists, I want to say, enables each to identify blind spots in the other while it disables each side from discerning them in itself. This is so because each side thinks that this is an ambiguity to be resolved rather than acknowledged and expressed in the institutional life. So where normalization proceeds relentlessly, the individualist will tend to convert certain of its results into elements appropriate to the very identity of the healthy, normal agent, and the communalist will select others to be ingredients in the good life we seek in common. Together they screen out too much of the politics of normalization.

To articulate this thesis further it will be helpful to glance at a text on democracy written forty years ago when American democracy was perceived to be threatened externally by totalitarianism, when the need to come to terms with new features of internal normalization was clear, and when the dangers in the latter process were not yet blatant enough to move proponents to give too much ontological weight to the disciplines involved. I have in mind Carl Friedrich's magisterial text *The New Belief in the Common Man*.[4] Friedrich could be quite open about the relation between democracy and discipline within the confines of a set of structures that were becoming more encompassing internally and vulnerable externally; for the adverse effects of the process he recommended had not yet been experienced so concretely.

> And though we may yearn for the happy go lucky ways of a pastoral society, bringing up our children in such a spirit means putting them out of the society in which they are born. . . . We

---

3. I have in mind the recent work by Charles Taylor, *Philosophical Papers*, Vols. 1 and 2 (Cambridge: Cambridge University Press, 1982); Michael Sandel, *Liberalism and the Limits of Justice* (Cambridge: Cambridge University Press, 1982); and Alasdair MacIntyre, *After Virtue* (South Bend: University of Notre Dame Press, 1981).

4. *The New Belief in the Common Man* (Cambridge: Harvard University Press, 1942).

had better take heed, and look for an education which is progressive in the direction in which our society is progressing.[5]

In this new setting we must examine more intensely a set of issues that
every society must come to terms with in some way.

> Every society or group must achieve an appropriate discipline
> or perish. The essential difference lies in the ultimate objective:
> authoritarian discipline aims at obedience, while the free man's
> discipline aims at self-discipline . . .[6]

Friedrich is admirable in his refusal to transcendentalize the disciplinary process but, from the perspective to be defended here, too
uncritical in his eagerness to extend this discipline into new areas of
life. But once this combination is accepted he must finally come to terms
with how the norms and the disciplines maintaining them are to be
justified. And here the new belief in the common man is wheeled into
place.

> Ultimately we come back to what we pointed out earlier,
> namely that we are dealing here not with abstract principles but
> with a communal way of doing things, with a common mode of
> behavior or conduct. Any men who do not act in accordance
> with the common mode are outside the community, and hence
> are subject to quite different methods of treatment. . . . A
> breakdown in values may occur within a democratic community
> just as it does other communities. A continuous effort is needed
> to maintain the community's democratic behavior intact.[7]

Friedrich's blunt response to the problem of discipline within a highly
organized democracy is unlikely to be endorsed so overtly today. But
the response helps to mark that space inside modern democracy where
individuality intersects and contends with commonality and where
otherness in the self confronts pressures internalized by the self as the
drive to normalization.

If, as I have suggested, contemporary democratic theory tends to
obscure normalizing tendencies built into modern democratic practice,
where are the disciplines which foster and maintain these norms? They
are located below the threshold of practices incorporated into the logic
of democratic legitimation, or, perhaps, they are experienced more as
ontological and social preconditions of democratic life than as elements

5. Ibid., p. 287.
6. Ibid.
7. Ibid., p. 284.

Democracy and Normalization

built into the extension of normalization in a democratic world. The proliferation of dualities of normality (normal/abnormal, healthy/sick, rational/irrational, responsible/irresponsible, stable/unstable) correlates with the enlargement of those areas of life into which bureaucratically enforced norms have penetrated. The growth of the latter has been dramatic. By comparison, for instance, to a hundred years ago a much larger portion of the American population today is either employed in institutions whose primary purpose is to observe, control, correct, confine, reform, cure, or regulate other people (e.g., the police, the military, intelligence agencies, polling centers, reform schools, therapeutic centers, halfway houses, prisons, welfare agencies, nursing homes, juridical institutions) or is the object of these operations (e.g., illegal aliens, prisoners, tax evaders, dissidents, welfare recipients, delinquents, the mentally disturbed, the retarded, nursing-home clients, divorcees).

These institutional complexes are governed by diverse purposes. But, first (in line with Friedrich's injunction to achieve "appropriate discipline or perish"), each operationalizes standards through which a target population is defined, judged, helped, corrected, or punished; second, the dualities of normality each constitutes are in need of redemption by theories of rationality, agency, and responsibility; and, third, the complex of theoretically redeemed practices functions to enclose the normal individual within parameters of stability, responsibility, innocence, and merit. These disciplines help to constitute the contemporary self as an individual. And conduct severely out of sync with the standards of normal individuality is seen to reflect an incapacity in the self or a defect in its supporting social conditions. In either case the interpretation calls for new disciplines that establish greater harmony between the self and conventions governing the order.

I wish to say that the modern urge to establish airtight philosophies of rationality and subjectivity is the wish to harmonize these two elements in the democratic ideal, to show how the extension of commonality can coalesce with the encouragement of individuality. But the desire to establish the appearance of harmony in actual democracies or the possibility of it in ideal democracies suppresses the ambiguity in democracy itself. And the suppression of this ambiguity tends to license the insidious extension of normalization into new corners of life. We need a theory and practice of democracy that appreciates this element of disharmony. One that understands harmonization to be normalization. One that insists that normalization, while unavoidable and desirable to some degree, also inflicts wounds on life. When the wounds are exposed we are in a better position to reconsider the appropriate scope of normalization and to attain a more critical perspective on those characteristics of the order that propel its extension. But to say these things it is necessary to reconsider the ontological frame within which modern democratic theory has been located.

Democracy and Discordance

The politics of modern democracies revolve not so much around the extent to which life should be normalized as around the question as to which norms shall govern the extension of normalization. In these struggles the participation of those already defined as severely abnormal tends to be discredited or disallowed. The irony of a normalizing democracy is that its projection of participation (or consent or even sometimes rights) into new areas tends to be accompanied by the marginalization of new sectors of the population or newly defined sectors of the self.

The modern effort to redeem standards of normality encourages those in pursuit of redemption to support a social ontology that converts boundaries and standards central to modern life into precepts of rationality, morality, or self-realization. These recipes for secular redemption cover up ambiguities inside democratic life. By making disciplines appear to be natural or rational or fulfilling they suppress the element of artificiality, unreason, and arbitrariness contained within them. They contribute in this way to the de-democratization of democracy.

By "social ontology" I mean a set of fundamental understandings about the relations of humans to themselves, to others, and to the world. An Aristotelian ontology understands the world to be a place where human beings can, when their common life is properly constituted, realize the telos appropriate to them. A Christian view construes the world and its "creatures" to be created by God; it defines the issues of life in terms of the proper relation of creatures to their creator.

The social ontology sustaining modern democracy has a trunk with two main branches. The trunk is formed by the principle of a subject realizing its essence in a larger world. The principle of subjectivity expresses the double faith that knowledge, action, and moral standards flow from a privileged center of agency and that this center can be redeemed by a transcendental argument showing it to be a necessary presupposition of life. The individualist branch locates subjectivity in the self; its medium is the interests, rights, responsibilities, and knowledge of individual subjects. The communal branch privileges the community or the intersubjective background in which life is situated; its medium is those virtues and identifications linking the individual to the larger whole. Hobbes, Locke, Kant, and Rawls represent powerful proponents of the first position, though most of them find it necessary to give some place to features in the second. Rousseau, Marx, Dewey, and Habermas give primacy to the second, though most of them incorporate significant elements from the first into their theories. Debates between them consist largely in each side trying to show how the other necessarily presupposes elements of the opposing theory to sustain itself. The current debate between civic republicans such as Charles Taylor, Michael Sandel, and Alasdair MacIntyre and individualists such as Ronald Dworkin and John Rawls exhibits these characteristics, though each side incorporates more features from the other than was the case with the majority of their classic predecessors. Having participated in such debates, I do not wish to discount their importance. But the terms of the established debate do obscure affinities between the adversaries in need of attention.

Each theory gravitates toward an ontology of concord. That is, each assumes that when properly constituted and situated the individual or collective subject achieves harmony with itself and with the other elements of social life. Thus any otherness discerned in the actual world becomes a sign that the selves in which it is located are incapacitated or that there is unintegrated material in need of assimilation or that the community needs to be broadened to internalize that which is now external to it. Otherness, the opponents agree, is something to be corrected, eliminated, punished, or integrated. The issue between them is how normalization is to proceed. Otherness—that which does not fit neatly into the form assumed by self or society—is not treated as that which might not fit because even a good order (or self) must itself produce elements that do not synchronize with its structure. It is never defined as worthy of respect in its very difference from the identity or good given primacy by the order or the theory in question.

A theory that must constantly define otherness as incapacity or a need requiring communal response or a sign that the communal terms of integration must be reformed lends too much ontological significance to the politics of normalization.

This characterization of commonality between two contending theories exaggerates. I mean to point to complementary tendencies linking opposing parties rather than to a monolithic drive uniting secret allies. The tendencies reside within texts and practices; they are less often explicit themes defended by them. And, as we shall see, there are also subversive tendencies in these same texts and practices to which I propose to give greater legitimacy. These subversive tendencies deserve greater prominence because they provide a counter to the politics of de-democratization built into the normalizing practices of democracy.

The relation between modern democratic theory and an ontology of concord is best brought out by contrasting the latter to an ontology of discordance or necessary dissonance within concord. The philosophy of discordance allows a place for the pursuit of personal and common identity while it strives to subdue the politics of normalization.

The latter philosophy refuses to postulate actual or potential identity among the elements constituting the self or the society. It expects discordance to be lodged in every unity achieved or discovered. And it discerns within the modern quest for identity the secularization of traditional religious impulses: devout secularists convert the creationist ontology into one which relocates unity and creativity in individual or collective subjects or in a pluralism which harmonizes these interdependent dimensions.

An ontology of discordance identifies some forms of otherness as the unavoidable effect of socially engendered harmonies. That which is recalcitrant or subjugated or excluded may be a sign that any human construct worthy of admiration must spawn that which does not fit. When we conclude that otherness (dirt, things out of place, unreason, mystery, eccentricity, instability) is itself produced by the artifices through which we complete ourselves, we are in a position to reconsider politically established orientations to these de-formations. We place ourselves in a position to discern and combat that side of democratic idealism which tends to equate good citizenship with normalization or to identify radical critique of an existing order with the aspiration to propel more inclusive forms of selfhood and community into being. We open ourselves to a philosophy that seeks, even in its commitment to the common good, to establish more space for otherness to be. And that sensibility better prepares us to uncover the pressures to normalize built into the structure of contemporary political economies.

The first question a normalizing democrat (or rationalist or moralist) poses when confronted with the ontology of discordance is, "How could it validate itself if its own formulation corrodes every ethic and theory of truth?" And the first and last answer the questioner typically accepts, "It cannot and therefore it is a self-refuting theory to be eliminated from the ranks of viable candidates for consideration." I do not now intend to respond in detail to this all too familiar question and

Democracy and Normalization

answer, though I have dealt with them elsewhere.[8] I think, indeed, that the charge of incoherence itself expresses a contestable faith in the sufficiency of the knowing enterprise; it presumes that since cognitive orientations to communication presuppose the redeemability of truth claims, no rhetorical strategy operating on the edge of this circle of cognition could call this faith into question. Here, however, we will consider two different questions. First, what philosophers have articulated an ontology of discordance and what effect does it have on the appearance presented by democratic practice? Second, is it possible to defend democratic institutions while endorsing such a philosophy and, if so, what alterations in the theory and practice of democracy are suggested by resituating them in this setting?

It may appear that Hobbesian philosophy expresses an appreciation of discordance. The self is at war with itself and often at odds with the dictates of reason and order. But every move Hobbes makes in his theory of self to support such a perspective is redefined in the theories of reason, sovereignty, and God. Hobbesian political theology grounds itself upon faith in divine providence in the last instance. It counsels humans limited by sinful dispositions and by partiality in their reasoning to treat the mysteries of life as signs of the omnipotence of their creator. There is a modest effort in Hobbes's thought to give space to difference when it does not interfere with the dictates of order. But the doctrine of reason as the human window onto God's will and commands absorbs the initial appearance of discordance into a higher concordance imposed upon humans through reason. Though resistance will persist in the rational order, it is always a sign of sin or irrationality in need of correction. Hobbes is a theorist of political conflict but not of discordance lodged within order and rationality.

Nietzsche is the modern thinker of significance who first explores such a perspective relentlessly. William James articulates some of its characteristics in his philosophy of radical empiricism. And Michel Foucault gives it a contemporary expression. But the first saw democracy only as a vehicle of weakness and resentment; the second did not explore the political implications of his thought; and the third was wary of its contribution to normalization.

We can glimpse the idea of discordance in this formulation by Nietzsche: "What alone can our teaching be? That no-one *gives* a human being his qualities: not God, not society, not his parents, not his ancestors, not he himself. . . . He is not the result of a special design, a

---

8. See "Taylor, Truth and Otherness" in *Political Theory* (August 1985) and Chapter 10 of the present volume.

will, a purpose."[9] The human is the incomplete animal, completed only within the frame of social form. But since humans were not designed to fit neatly into any social form, and since no ideal form has been predesigned to mesh with every drive and stirring within the self, every particular form of completion subjugates even while it realizes something in us, does violence to selves even while enabling them to be. It is this ambiguous relation between our need for completion and the arbitrary element within any actual completion that leads Nietzsche to characterize the human as "the sick animal." Our resentment against discordance and finitude encourages us to create compensatory philosophies of concordance. And the quest for concordance through the containment or assimilation or conquest of otherness exacerbates this sickness.

The politics of insidious assimilation flows most dramatically from the effort to improve the self by drawing it closer to its true self or final essence. Foucault, the genealogist of modernity as the normalizing society, states this theme in the following way: "One might say that the ancient right to *take* life or *let* live was replaced by a power to *foster* life or disallow it to the point of death." Power in the old regimes "was essentially a right of seizure: of things, time, bodies, and ultimately life itself; it culminated in the privilege to seize life in order to suppress it." Much of life existed outside or on the margins of power, and power entered into life whenever it overstepped its prescribed limits. As power shifts from protecting sovereign prerogatives to enabling life to realize its potentialities within a well-ordered society, power becomes more constitutive (more "productive") in character. It now works to "incite, reinforce, control, optimize, and organize the forces under it: a power bent on generating forces, making them grow, and ordering them, rather than one dedicated to impeding them, making them submit or destroying them."[10]

While modern philosophies of self and society compete to give the right purposes to these optimizing forces, they coalesce to obscure the way in which optimizing power normalizes. Normalization is further abetted by the modern shift in the locus of sovereignty from the ruler to the people. For power now serves the people itself. This tightening of the web of power culminates in the new shape of war. "Wars are no longer waged in the name of a sovereign who must be defended; they are waged on behalf of the existence of everyone. . . . The atomic situa-

9. *Twilight of the Idols*, trans. R. J. Hollingdale (New York: Penguin Books, 1968), p. 54.
10. *The History of Sexuality*, Vol. 1, trans. Robert Hurley (New York: Vintage Press, 1980), pp. 138, 136.

tion is now at the end point of this process: the power to expose a whole population to death is the underside of the power to guarantee an individual's continued existence."[11]

Foucault is ambivalent about democracy, suggesting that since every order requires boundaries and limits, democratic procedures may be the best way to establish them after all. But Nietzsche's hostility contains no apparent ambivalence. Democracy is the triumph of weakness over strength; it expresses the triumph of resentment over the affirmation of life in its discordance and finitude; it gives the "herd" hegemony over that which would deviate from it. But I believe Foucault and Nietzsche overlooked certain ingredients in democratic practice expressive of the essential tension between the need for commonality and the need to respond to the ways in which commonality subjugates. Perhaps they did so because the dimension of democracy most attuned to the element of discordance within concord has periodically found a more robust expression in America than in Europe.

A political theory attuned to discordance lodged within the concordance between thought and unthought, word and thought, word and thing, mood and its articulation, common good and the good of particular selves, personal identities socially redeemed and that in the self subdued by such redemption, the imperatives of the present and the needs of the future, the desire for transcendental reassurance and the indifference of the world to that desire—a political theory attentive to such discordance will find a highly congenial strain within the ambiguous legacy of democracy. This strain will be given its due only when the strife, recalcitrance, and dissimulation within democratic politics is treated as part of the affirmation of life itself, and that orientation will be possible only to the degree that the imperatives of modern political economies are relaxed to establish more space for discordance to be, without disrupting the necessary limits of order.

Thus Spoke Zarathustra can be read as a series of dialogues between Zarathustra and his animals, the soothsayer, the ugliest man, the old woman, the higher men, etc.; it can also be read as a plurality of voices in Zarathustra jostling for a hearing. It is a book for "everyone and no-one" because each of us contains disturbing voices within the plurality available to us and few of us are willing to allow these disturbances to find expression. Because we yearn for a world in which our finitude is redeemed and in which suffering is shown to serve some higher purpose, we are inclined to give hegemony to these voices of reassurance. To be weak is to close off the voices of discordance within the self; it is

11. Ibid. p. 136.

also to demand punishment of those whose discordant articulations create disturbance in oneself.

Democracy, when it is not enveloped in the ontological tissue of concordance or bound by the chains of economic rationality, is a medium through which these voices of otherness can find expression in the self and the public world.

Democratic life is, first, the medium through which any self can wage its own struggle between weakness and strength. If the self is the locus of strife between the quest for transcendental purpose in life and the affirmation of life without such purpose, between revenge against temporality and affirmation of finitude, between silencing the disturbance of otherness and accepting it as a spur to the self, and if economic class, birth, gender, or formal education do not suffice to differentiate weakness from strength, then democratic turbulence—the politics that unsettles the settled—enables this struggle to be waged within anyone and everyone. It exposes any self to the possibility of affirming life amidst its discordances; it thus encourages greater acceptance of otherness in oneself and other selves. There should be, indeed, ample space for debate between alternative interpretations of what the struggle is and how to wage it. For many would revise the definitions of "weakness" and "strength" endorsed here. But as long as the definitions advanced here have some presence in the public life, democratic practice still emerges as the best medium through which each can confront the disturbance posed by otherness to the self.

Democratic practice is, second, the best way, particularly when a range of citizens acknowledges this internal strife, to define the limits, norms, and ends appropriate to the common life. If any self is incomplete without social form and if any good social form realizes some things in the self by subordinating others, democratic politics allows a common good to be defined while also enabling the dirt within it to find expression. Democratic politics of the sort endorsed here does not eliminate the need for norms. It insists upon it. But when conditions are right, and when a sufficient number of citizens have affirmed discordance as part of the human condition, democratic turbulence subdues the politics of normalization. It supports the ambiguous relation to public life essential to freedom. It—again when it is freed from the shackles of concordant ontology—expresses the ambiguity lodged in its own mode of politics without giving too much ontological weight to the social requirements of normalization.

This, again, is a radical idealization of democracy. Rather, it is a double idealization. It accentuates tendencies in democratic practice worthy of glorification and then dissociates them from ontologies of concordance that obscure the violence in normalization. It concentrates attention on the persistent ambiguity between the democratic appreciation of individuality and its drive to extend popular control over common areas of life, between its appreciation of agency and its tendency to convert social norms into definitional preconditions of agency, between the human drive to have settled expectations and the need to expose the dirt buried within them. By enabling its own ambiguity to become more overt it encourages us to be wary of doctrines that glorify normalization by defining it as harmonization; it encourages us to treat normalization as an ambiguous good to be qualified, countered, and politicized.

A theory of democracy located in an ontology of discordance will idealize politics. Politics, at its best, is the medium through which essential ambiguities can be expressed and given some redress. It is simultaneously the best way to establish or confirm commonalities and to expose uncertainties, repressed voices, exclusions, and injuries lodged within them. Politics, again at its best, calls into question settlements sedimented into moral consensus, economic rationality, administrative procedure, legal propriety, psychiatric judgment, and ontological necessity. It enables cherished media of harmonization such as the self as subject, economic growth as a fundamental component of the good life, and the indispensability of political authority to be experienced simultaneously as mechanisms of normalization and as vehicles of realization.

Under the right conditions, then, democracy politicizes and politics democratizes. The problem is to identify the right conditions and to recognize those features of contemporary life that now militate aginst their consolidation. That, at least, is an agenda for those of us who wish to situate democracy within a philosophy of dissonant holism.

2

THE POLITICS OF

REINDUSTRIALIZATION

The Threat to the Welfare State

The fragile consensus that sustained expansion of the American welfare state for forty-five years has now dissolved. Many see the achievements of the welfare state as a nightmare; and no liberal is now prepared to argue that a new version of the New Deal, Fair Deal, New Frontier, or Great Society can be developed and packaged for use during the next presidential campaign. The official debate revolves not around the question of whether to contract the relative size of the welfare state, but rather around where and how to cut the "fat" out of public spending for civilian programs.

The sources of public disaffection from the welfare state are numerous. But one source, coming as a surprise to most liberals, deserves special notice. A variety of recent welfare programs and clients, spawned between 1960 and 1980, pose a threat to the self-identity of traditional welfare-state supporters who are white, earn relatively modest incomes, have fairly steady jobs, and live family-centered lives. While the latter group continued to benefit from a variety of programs, the effect of the new policies on their sense of dignity and self-respect rendered many of them extremely ambivalent about the size of the state, its role in the economy, and its effectiveness in carrying out its ascribed role. These vulnerable constituencies did not need too much political coaxing to bite the hand that had slapped them in the face.

If a person's identity is centered on the relation between work and family; if one believes (or, better, struggles to believe) that one bears a large share of credit or blame for the kind of person one becomes, the character one develops, the income one earns, the values endorsed by one's children, and the opportunities placed within their reach, then public programs and rhetoric that jeopardize this identity will be construed as attacks on the self one has become. Thus, if school busing for purposes of racial integration disconnects the school from the neighborhood, parents lose the ability to influence through housing decisions and local participation the kind of education their children will receive. The sense of self-reliance on the part of one constituency is sacrificed to the effort to provide equal opportunity for another. If welfare programs are extended to new groups on the grounds that individuals are not personally responsible for their dependency, working men and women can no longer take much personal credit for the independence they have achieved. If women and minorities are given special breaks in landing the small number of good jobs available on the grounds that they have been discriminated against historically, white, male, lower-and middle-class workers are made to feel that they deserve to be stuck in the lowly jobs they now have. Seen from the perspective of these latter constituencies *everyone else* is now treated either as meritorious or as unjustly closed out from the ranks of the meritorious. If ecologists demand policies that appear to threaten the jobs or limit the consumption possibilities of blue-collar workers, environmentalism is likely to be seen as one of the privileges of the privileged classes. If liberals and radicals respond to rising crime rates with rehabilitation proposals for criminals and gun-control legislation for everyone else, the breadwinner's self-restraint in abiding by the law begins to look foolish, and his sense of helplessness in the face of criminal assault is enhanced. And if taxes on working people are increased for the apparent purpose of promoting these policy objectives, they are doubly assaulted: they are asked to pay for programs that invalidate the sense of dignity, self-reliance, and responsibility available to them in the current order.

The perception informing each of these liberal initiatives has of course been correct. Minorities and women do face unwarranted discrimination; unemployment, poverty, and underemployment are rooted in structural defects in the political economy; street crime is bred by the conditions of existence in the underclass; the environment is ravaged by the patterns of production and consumption that prevail in America. But these perceptions, formed within the network of assumptions and priorities that constitute the welfare state, have also filtered out the ways in which the programs selected to redress these evils demean a large class of citizens who face their own insecurities and anxieties in contemporary America.

The welfare liberalism of the past few decades has been blind to the disjuncture between the sense of injustice many Americans feel when confronted with the plight of excluded minorities and the hostility they feel toward the specific public remedies for that injustice. This blindness has helped to set up the welfare state to be the principal object of public disaffection and to give the New Right a moral advantage in the competition for public support.

The persistence of wide support for Social Security confirms this reading. The Social Security system faces serious problems of equity as well as finance. It takes a large and visible chunk from the weekly paycheck of the worker; it is even possible that those paying into it today will not receive a comparable return tomorrow. But public acceptance is still intact because the program is designed to support all participants and because the participants believe that the current beneficiaries have earned their benefits through a lifetime of work. The fiscal crisis of this system has not produced a political crisis because it coheres with standards of justice and dignity shared by participants.

Welfare-state liberalism emerged as a series of responses to defects and injustices in the development of capitalism. Inspired by democratic sentiments, it defined itself against certain effects of capitalist development: against its cycles of inflation and unemployment, its ruthless treatment of those who could not fit into its shifting standards of success, its destruction of the natural supports of human life, its tendencies to close many out of effective citizenship. The natural adversary of welfarism is the philosophy of unfettered market competition, a philosophy that minimizes the role of the state except in the areas of military development and internal security.

Welfarists shared with marketeers a commitment to the priority of economic growth. The welfare state cannot accumulate the revenues it needs to redress the adverse effects of private enterprise unless the private system provides it with a large tax dividend; and the tax dividend depends on the success of economic expansion in the private sector. The welfare state is thus deeply dependent on the system it seeks to regulate; it must subsidize and nourish the private economy even while it strives to tame and regulate it. This ambiguous relation goes a long way toward explaining why the attempts of the welfare state to secure justice produced effects that eventually eroded the support of needed constituencies.

This structural ambiguity could go largely unnoticed during an earlier period because the ideal of the universalization of private affluence then seemed inherently more realizable than it seems today. The state did not seem locked into the pursuit of growth; that pursuit seemed to be tied to its effort to support the quest for private affluence and to rectify the accompanying injustices.

These two goals encouraged welfarists to adopt some of the most fundamental assumptions and priorities of their major political adversaries. These were not topics for debate but common premises from which the debate proceeded. The terms of debate that favored welfarism during four decades of state expansion now place it in a defensive posture. Today the connection between liberalism and welfarism threatens to suffocate the most humane commitments that have energized both.

The major threat to welfare liberalism does not now come from its traditional adversary, the marketeers, but from the new ideology of reindustrialization. The doctrine was first outlined in a *Business Week* issue modestly calling for the "reindustrialization of America";[1] it has received more evangelical treatment in George Gilder's *Wealth and Poverty*.[2] The two statements complement each other, the first developing aspects of the doctrine that will appeal to managerial elites and the second adding those that will mesmerize partisans of the Moral Majority.[3] The two texts together avoid many of the pitfalls into which marketeers have repeatedly stumbled in their debates with welfarists. The reindustrialists, for instance, are wary of monetarism because it often works to stifle private investment and industrial expansion. Unlike the marketeers, the new industrialists openly support a positive role for the state in the economy, not in aiding the poor or protecting the natural environment, but in subsidizing the private expansionary process. They demand tax reform, not to redistribute income from the rich to the poor, but to free investment by the rich. They acknowledge that the escalating defense budget is inflationary but accept this as a necessary burden to be borne by the leader of the free world. They don't worry too much about deficit spending by the state as long as its predominant purpose is to expand long-term productive capacity in the private sector. They are not concerned about monopolistic or oligopolistic corporations. Even if one unit dominates a product field, the possibility of entry by a new competitor will goad the giant to maintain efficiency and cost effectiveness. And—finally—the point where sibling rivalry between reindustrialists and marketeers becomes most pronounced: the new industrialists do not view inflation as the most fundamental social evil to be avoided; inflation becomes a virtue when it supports a new burst of industrial expansion and the redistribution of income toward the upper levels of the economy.

The reindustrialists outbid the marketeers and welfarists in their

1. June 30, 1980.
2. New York: Basic Books, 1980.
3. *Business Week* confirms this connection, saying that "*Wealth and Poverty* is indispensable for anyone who wishes to understand the intellectual basis for widespread changes that have already altered the direction of American politics and will help shape public policy in the 1980s" (December 29, 1980). I suspect that often Gilder supports proposals—especially with respect to the poor—that *Business Week* cannot officially endorse but that cohere with their desire to subordinate all other concerns to the overriding priority of industrial expansion and economic growth.

devotion to economic growth; they insist that it be given the highest priority. The state must exercise new initiatives (including those opposed by market monetarists) and eliminate unproductive subsidies (primarily those traditionally supported by welfarists) in pursuing this objective.

Reindustrialists are single-minded, and that may eventually be their undoing. They have gained the upper hand today because of the dazzling future they promise, their ability to shed some of the most obvious liabilities of the traditional market vision of the economy, the failure of welfarists to sustain high rates of growth, and the rancor many people feel toward the most visible programs of the welfare state. The reindustrialists will probably fail in getting large parts of their program through or fail in obtaining the promised results from those parts of the program enacted. But their failure will not suffice to return welfarism to power. Reindustrialization today stands to welfarism as the New Deal did to the laissez-faire perspective in the 1930s. Even its failures will look positive by comparison with the discredited alternatives posed by its demoralized adversaries. Welfarists are today reduced to opposing reindustrialization programs with abstract expressions of "compassion for the poor and the needy." And many old welfarists are eagerly developing their own more modest versions of reindustrialization.

The reindustrialists themselves devote most of their attention to the *incentives* they hope to initiate on the supply side of the economy to spur private investment, work effort, productivity, economic growth, and a more favorable position in the international economy. They would curtail business regulation ("deregulation"), subsidize businesses with a promising future in the international economy, reduce taxes on capital and savings, increase depreciation allowances, decontrol oil and natural gas prices, subsidize a shift from oil to coal, give private management more help in improving worker productivity, and sharply increase military production. The result, it is claimed, will be a more productive economy, eventual improvements in the standard of living for productive Americans, and an expanded military establishment that will assure the flow of essential foreign resources into the American economy. Indeed, what the reindustrialists now say the economy needs to spur growth is approximately what, for decades, a set of neo-Marxists have prophesied would emerge as the new imperatives of advanced capitalism.[4]

4. I have in mind primarily the studies by James O'Connor, *The Fiscal Crisis of the State* (New York: St. Martin's Press, 1973), and Jürgen Habermas, *Legitimation Crisis* (Boston: Beacon Press, 1973).

Even the incentive side of the program imposes harsh sacrifices on constituencies that have recently gained an insecure foothold within the American system. Merely consider some of the complaints about government regulation advanced by the editors of *Business Week*. The problem with the Foreign Corrupt Practices Act is that it "severely limits corporate payments of fees to obtain contracts abroad." Trade embargoes launched on behalf of human rights "limit sales of grain and high technology equipment to the East bloc." The Nuclear Proliferation Treaty "limits exports of nuclear reactors and materials to countries that might produce a bomb." Human rights policy "limits trade with certain countries that violate human rights cases." Antitrust laws "prohibit U.S. corporations from establishing joint trading companies." Health, safety, and environmental regulations increase domestic costs of compliance and "enforce strict U.S. standards for overseas operations of U.S. companies." The incentives devised to reindustrialize thereby insinuate a series of profound moral reversals into the normal operation of the political economy. The old taboos become the new virtues.

But the incentive proposals are matched by a further set of sacrifices and disciplines to be imposed on those who are superfluous to the reindustrialization game plan or without the strategic location needed to resist it effectively. The call for selective sacrifice is now couched within the traditional language of a social contract to which all rational parties ought to consent. We need, they say, a "remodeling . . . of the social contract," one that reflects the "understanding that our common interest in returning the country to a path of strong economic growth overrides other conflicting interests." Some of the signatories are asked to scale down the inflated expectations they have developed over the past two decades. Too much has been expected of the civilization of productivity. It has been asked to "support an ever rising standard of living; create endless jobs; provide education, medical care and housing for everyone; abolish poverty; rebuild the cities; restore the environment; satisfy the demands of blacks, Hispanics, women and other groups."[5]

Some of these demands must be delayed; others must be forgotten. For the next decade or so the whole society must shift its priorities from consumption to investment. Workers must scale their wage demands to the rate of increase in productivity. Welfare recipients, at least in Gilder's version of the doctrine, must receive lower levels of support so that welfare will become "unattractive and even a bit demeaning."[6] The excessive concern with "quality of life" issues (pollution, toxic

5. *Business Week*, June 30, 1980.
6. *Wealth and Poverty*, p. 117.

wastes, health and safety on the job, the integrity of the natural environment, the safety and quality of products on the market) must be deflated. Rational modes of work organization and control must be extended into the upper reaches of private and public employment so that these tasks emulate "the cognitive style of the industrialist instead of the humanist."[7] The state must resist the urge to aid old cities and old industries, allowing surplus residents to migrate to more promising areas. Finally, those at the bottom of the income-security hierarchy must give up the dream of a more egalitarian society; able-bodied men and women stuck at the bottom must "work harder than the classes above them" in order for some of them "to move up" into a higher position in a stratification system that itself must be extended rather than contracted. Because the "average worker exerts himself at half-capacity" he must do better than he has in the past, while low-income workers, trying to improve their lot, must do considerably better than the new average.

Clearly the new social contract contains a new set of asymmetrical agreements. One set of signatories—such as high-technology industries, the military-industrial complex, workers in growth industries, and residents in western and southern states—are to consent to a new set of incentives; while others—such as low-income workers, urban residents in the frost belt, minorities, women in lower and middle levels of the work force, environmentalists, liberal-arts educators, public-sector employees in nonmilitary areas, welfare recipients, civilian retirees, the unemployed, the sick, the mentally ill, and the maladjusted—are asked to bear up under new burdens and constraints. Not only will particular constituencies be unimpressed with these contract proposals, but most citizens will be adversely affected by the changes in their daily lives accompanying deregulation.

Surely the reindustrialists suspect that some parties to this contract will sign only under duress. The legitimacy of the civilization of productivity has been based largely on its promise to bring all members of society into the charmed circle of private affluence while preserving democratic citizenship, the quality of the natural environment, the right to a decent education, and a dignified life for old people. We are now informed, and rather casually at that, that growth is still the means and consumption the name of the good life, but that the means necessitate exclusion of many from the rewards. The end of growth is no longer the universalization of affluence, but selective austerity, intensification of social discipline, and a deteriorating natural and social environment. The new captains of industry are relentless.

7. Ibid., p. 211.

Do the ideologists of reindustrialization expect those who did not draft this new contract to consent to it voluntarily? Or do they have other ways in mind of converting this contract proposal into an offer the losers can't refuse?

Well, the reindustrialists contend that it is rational for all parties to sign because no alternative scenario can cope with the problems of unemployment, inflation, stagnation, and worker motivation that plague the economy. When one looks closely, though, it becomes clear that the captains of industry expect some constituencies to resist the needed disciplines. They have techniques available to help those who at first do not heed the voice of reason to meet their social responsibilities. Fortunately for the new industrialists, those most in need of disciplinary control are also those who have the least market and political leverage in the American political economy. Several disciplinary techniques can be applied in a setting where the current alternatives to reindustrialization have been discredited by historical experience.

First, tax revolts will work wonders. As citizens react to high taxes, large portions of which are ticketed for business subsidies, highway expenditures, and the military, or are designed to rectify the adverse social effects of private productivity, the state will cut back services and support to those clients with the weakest political leverage. The cutbacks will thus fit broadly into the pattern recommended by the reindustrialists. It will shift resources from unproductive to productive activities.

Second, once the reindustrial agenda is launched, inflation itself can be deployed to redistribute burdens and benefits in the desired directions. Inflation is an acceptable tool to reindustrialists since "most of the greatest episodes of economic history—from the commercial revolution to the industrial revolution—occurred in the midst of rising prices and rising debts."[8] It is not inflation but the purpose it serves that is crucial to this scenario:

> If the United States diverts the proceeds of its inflation tax into the creative core of capitalist growth—the new research and industry of the future—both the problem of inflation and the problem of growth will disappear. If we continue to subsidize the dying parts of the economy and the deadening growth of bureaucracy, inflation and torpor will persist regardless of all the heroic discipline of debt and money.[9]

8. Ibid., p. 229.
9. Ibid., p. 231.

When inflation occurs, workers in the more productive industries can be allowed to bargain for higher wages. But those with less leverage in the public sector, in less productive private industries, and in nonunion market firms can be held back. And the state, in the name of efficiency, can refuse to index welfare, retirement, and Medicaid payments to the rate of inflation. Inflation thus contains creative potential for disciplinary control of selected constituencies. Artfully deployed, it can divide people by class, market location, generation, and regional location, and it can redistribute income and wealth from the lower toward the upper end of the continuum. Moreover, because the distributive effects of inflation are not so directly attributable to public decisions, they can to some degree be produced without public identification of political responsibility. Anyway, this, I think, is the hope lurking between the lines of the reindustrialization texts.

Third, the welfare apparatus of the state need not be dismantled completely; that would deprive the state of a depository of disciplinary controls to be employed in the cause of reindustrialization. For the agencies that provide services to clients also provide centers for state surveillance and management of the dependent clientele. It is unlikely that most agencies will meet the fate of those specifically entrusted with the regulation of business (e.g., the Environmental Protection Agency and the Occupational Safety and Health Administration). In other cases, where the primary contact is with welfare recipients, teenagers, delinquents, criminals, and the maladjusted, the police function of the agencies will be extended and tightened, and welfare services will be reduced to the minimum level needed to maintain contact with the client populations.

Implicit in the explicit call for a new social contract is the real message of reindustrialization: despite more than a hundred years of capital accumulation, the old promises on behalf of the productive society can no longer be made. The plan to reindustrialize America contains the implicit admission that the effort did not work as expected the first time around. It must be planned both more restrictively and more comprehensively the second time through—restrictively with respect to the beneficiaries to be drawn in by incentives and promises for a better future, comprehensively with respect to the modes of disciplinary control to be imposed on those to whom present incentivies cannot be given or promises made with credibility.

If the program for the reindustrialization of America were converted into practice, it would mean the de-democratization of America. For it would place the most crucial economic decisions beyond the reach of public accountability and would shunt constituencies and public needs that do not fit into the reindustrialization syndrome toward the margins of economic life and social legitimacy. If reindustrialization gains hegemony, public elections will persist. But the range of options debated will be narrow, and the state's capacity to discipline those who do not exercise self-discipline will be extended. A number of cautious journalists and social scientists, predictably, will ignore the gap between the production of social evils and the generation of legitimate issues. They will continue to cultivate a studied innocence about the historical course we are on by *equating* democratic politics with electoral competition.

Defanging Reindustrialization

What are the alternative visions to reindustrialization now that welfarism has been pushed into a defensive posture? One is the politics of radical protest spawned during the 1960s and showing signs of revival today. But protest politics flourishes best when it faces a healthy liberal establishment that believes that justice and the good life can be fostered by the welfare state. As long as the liberal doctrine retained a powerful presence in our politics, particularly as long as it celebrated the progressive possibilities within the order, radical protest could hope to mobilize liberal efforts to prove that space for progressive action actually existed. The liberals made promises on behalf of that order; dissident pressures then compelled them to recognize injustices previously hidden and to find ways to live up to the promises they had made. It was a cozy relationship of mutuality and interdependence, even if neither party identified as many virtues in its partner as it found in itself.

If the decline of welfare liberalism proceeds very far, the next wave of radical protests—provoked by foreign adventurism or by the new disciplines imposed by reindustrialization—are likely to provide a pretext for repressive responses by the state, and the measures may well be legitimized by the larger populace. If the protests disturb the progress of reindustrialization in a setting where its premises and priorities have filtered into the old liberal doctrine, the protests will appear to undercut the only rational response available to the issues facing the country. The legitimacy of the protests will be undercut by the weakened credibility of welfare liberalism and the state will be empowered to put them down in the name of reason. When the liberal host becomes sick the radical parasite is not apt to remain healthy either.

The emergence of reindustrialization thus demands a reconstitution of liberalism and a redefinition of the priorities and strategies of radicalism. The reconstitution must acknowledge the moment of truth in the widespread disaffection from the welfare state; it must reaffirm the respect for political democracy, human dignity, and an inclusive economic life that has animated most radicals and liberals in the modern era; and it must reconsider the fundamental economic premises and priorities that have governed American liberalism, at least from the era of the New Deal to that of the Moral Majority. The comments that follow are designed to contribute some ideas to the dialogue to be pursued.

The commitments welfarists have shared historically with their market adversaries are those most in need of reassessment. The idea that public support of private economic growth would provide the populace with steadily increasing affluence, happiness, freedom, and security now seems questionable in the light of both recent historical experience and mainstream projections concerning the future of the civilization of productivity. More pertinent to liberal welfarism itself, the idea that public support of rapid growth in the privately incorporated economy would generate a tax dividend to be used to rectify the adverse "side effects" (the phrase reveals how marginal these effects were presumed to be) of that growth now needs reconsideration. The agenda has placed welfare liberalism in the defensive posture it now finds itself. For the new captains of industry are more relentlessly committed to the common priority of growth, and they can now blame the inflated size of the state budget for the hardships that face the economy. Today, commitment to the priority of growth *is* commitment to the intensification of discipline and selective austerity; liberals who continue to give primacy to the first end will eventually be drawn into complicity with the means to its realization. The point is, first, to communicate this fact politically to people whose daily experience already validates it, and, second, to show how persisting features of the political economy that now lock the populace into the illusory pursuit of growth can be reconstituted.

There are many sources of the growth imperative, but one of them is particularly important for those who seek to accentuate democratic control over the political economy. For it explains why the populace allows itself to be drawn into the orbit of the growth syndrome even though its own experience increasingly reveals the illusions inside the pursuit. The patterns of consumption that prevail in the United States establish the appearance of affluence while they increase the difficulties many individuals and families face in making ends meet. People cannot meet the costs of housing, energy, transportation, education, health, insurance, private security, taxation, retirement, cultural life, and recreation without the promise of a steady increase in income levels. They cannot do so because the social infrastructure of consumption in the affluent society progressively converts former luxuries and privileges into imperatives of consumption. Political support for the priority of growth is mobilized by constant pressure on the family budget generated by these changes in the infrastructure of consumption; and the direction in which growth proceeds constantly generates new shifts in the infrastructure of consumption. By "the social infrastructure of consumption" I mean publicly and privately generated rules and effects that, in the strongest sense, allow some forms of consumption and disallow others and, in the weaker sense, encourage some forms while discouraging others. Examples: The publicly instituted highway system, in conjunction with the location of shopping malls, workplaces, and supermarkets, renders the automobile—along with its costs of purchase, fuel, insurance, maintenance, and periodic replacement—a necessity for participation in the common life of the society. Public and private energy policies make oil, natural gas, coal, and nuclear power necessary objects of consumption for most Americans. The organization of advertising makes it impossible to buy goods without paying expensive advertising costs. The shorter life of "durable goods" necessitates more frequent replacements over the life of one individual or family. A health insurance scheme that leaves fee-setting power in the hands of physicians while it partially collectivizes payment helps to generate a medical system that is expensive, dependent on high technology, and curative rather than preventative in its emphasis. Product "improvements" that complicate commodities (the car, household appliances) require special tools and skills for their repair and maintenance, and render more and more "handymen" unhandy. The social processes that generate high rates of crime increase private and public costs of security. Rules governing employment of the elderly increase private and public expenditures for retirement. Industrial production processes and product priorities produce new costs of securing clean air, pure water, fertile soil, and scenic beauty.

These examples merely illustrate ways in which shifts in the social infrastructure of consumption constantly expand the private expenditures and public tax levels required to allow a majority of the populace to participate in the common life available in the society.

The new captains of industry come close to acknowledging the logic of this negative dialectic and perilously close to lifting the cover of legitimacy off the civilization of productivity. For they now contend that the

economy that once promised to bring everyone within its circle of benefits and privileges must now promote growth by freezing large segments of society out of its paradigmatic benefits. One reindustrialist is
quite blunt about it:

> A decade of public and private belt-tightening is therefore
> needed if all the obsolescent elements are to be replaced and
> others adapted to the current environment: otherwise the slow
> economic growth, decline in productivity, inflationary pressure
> and other well known signs of the strained economy will per-
> sist. . . . If our industrial base is to grow along the lines I have
> outlined, public and private consumption must be sacrificed to
> some extent.[10]

The word has reached the apologists for the civilization of productivity,
though it is still stated timidly and without awareness of its historic
implications. The pursuit of private affluence through the expansion of
private capital does produce riches, but it also obstructs realization of
the good life that was supposed to accompany them. As the pursuit
continues, the end recedes; as the end recedes, the disciplines needed
to maintain the pursuit intensify. The end of growth is not fulfillment of
the dream of affluence. The moment for that dream has passed, though
many will strive to hang onto it for an hour or two longer. The old hope
can no longer inspire a vision of the common future we are building; it
can only inspire a yearning, a nostalgia, for a past condition in which
such a belief in that future was possible. And because the old end is
drained of its connection to the good life, it will be increasingly difficult
to mobilize workers, consumers, and dependents of the welfare state to
accept the new disciplines and sacrifices required to sustain it. A web of
covert evasions and resistances will continue to unfold—the emergence
of the "underground economy" is just one index of this phenomenon—
and private and public bureaucracies will try to penetrate more deeply
into the fabric of everyday life to contain these movements.

The hegemony of growth, reflected in the obeisance both major political parties give to it, is less and less sustained by popular belief in the
future it will foster; it is today sustained more by the social infrastructure of consumption that impels people to support official policies of
disciplinary control at the political level while they struggle to evade
them in private life. This picture of our condition is forming in the
minds of many Americans. But it will neither crystallize into a political

10. Amitai Etzioni, *New York Times*, June 29, 1980.

doctrine nor foster a progressive social movement until credible proposals to reconstitute this infrastructure are developed.

We can approach this challenge by considering the differences between exclusive and inclusive goods. An exclusive good cannot be extended to the populace as a whole without (1) decreasing the private value of the good to those who have already received it, (2) increasing the private costs of its use, (3) accentuating the adverse social effects of its use, and (4) increasing the costs borne by the state in trying to rectify these adverse effects. Inclusive goods reverse each of these effects. There are, certainly, few goods that fit within either category perfectly, but there are significant differences between alternative forms of transportation, housing, health care, food supply, and insurance. The universalization of the automobile, for instance, receives low grades on this scale by comparison to the universalization of rail, transit, and bus systems. Similarly, a medical system based on high technology and insurance payments to physicians who set their own fees is much more costly to extend to the entire populace than one organized around membership in a prepaid plan, preventive health care, and salaried medical staff. It might be said that the American civilization has been constructed around the illusory hope of universalizing exclusive goods, and that reindustrialization represents an attempt to restore the health of the economy by restricting a larger share of exclusive goods to a smaller proportion of the populace.

Inclusive goods promote an infrastructure of consumption that eases the *public* pressures for constant economic growth and incorporates more members into the good life it makes possible. The shift toward inclusive goods would thus support democratic practice in two ways: by easing the economic pressures that stifle public exploration of alternatives to reindustrialization, and by extending to all members the security and dignity needed for participation as citizens in the common life.

There are certainly other ingredients to be included in a post-welfare-state perspective on the democratic left. But, I believe, any such perspective must pay close attention to the intimate relations among the prevailing organization of consumption, the difficulties people face in making ends meet, the sources of disaffection from the welfare state, and the political appeal of reindustrialization. Perhaps the serious liabilities of reindustrialization can be exposed most dramatically by a perspective that articulates those connections politically and identifies ways to render our economic life more inclusive.

3

CIVIC DISAFFECTION AND

THE DEMOCRATIC PARTY

The Common Good and Its Devaluation

America, once hailed as the new world of riches and freedom, now presents itself as a nation simmering with undefined domestic ills and ominous military impulses. Even some of its most ardent defenders glimpse the new condition, if mainly through a glass, darkly. Neoconservatives trace our troubles to the rise of unreasonable expectations among spoiled citizens who refuse to accept limits necessary to the good life, while they attribute the rising tide of entitlements to the seductive influence of an intellectual class alienated from the achievements of modernity. The champions of "reindustrialization" accept and embellish this account. In their view, new obstacles to capital realization constitute the basic source of our troubles. While recognizing the passive resistance of workers, welfare recipients, and consumers to the new modes of mobilization, they treat it as a problem to be solved by managerial skill. Welfare liberals, oblivious until recently to the ground shifting beneath their feet, still hope that the collapse of the Reagan program will restore liberal compassion to public favor.

Each of these perspectives struggles to recapture a world we are losing, to rekindle a fading vision of the future promised by the society of riches. Each strategy of restoration, if it is to project the positive image desired, must silence deep doubts stirring in many circles and contain the expressions of disillusionment among subordinate constituencies asked to believe old promises while they bear new domestic burdens and foreign risks.

Walter Dean Burnham provides a more credible account of these troubles, and though he refuses to soften us up with contrived expressions of optimism, his interpretation may provide the ground for a new position to be established in the current political debate. Burnham contends that state priorities such as capital accumulation that might revitalize the economy are unable to secure the allegiance of a legion of nonvoters who resist the servile roles reserved for them in the neoconservative scenarios of sacrifice; while more compassionate programs, pursued by the liberal wing of the Democratic party, are unable to generate the broad coalition needed to enact them, to overcome roadblocks placed in their path by a variety of strategically located interests, or to sustain the rate of economic growth needed to protect their economic basis. We face "a general crisis of the regime as a whole," though its real character is not yet articulated in our political dialogue.[1]

One fears that if the current impasse persists, the frustrations and anxieties building within it will increase public tolerance for an extension of repressive controls over those who hamper the scenarios of the right. It becomes clear that the democratic left, currently out of touch with the party of nonvoters and out of favor with organized labor, must break new ground if it is to respond to these new circumstances. Since I concur with much of Burnham's account I will try first to develop some of its dimensions further and then ask what implications they might carry for a reconstitution of the democratic left.

Consider a list of phenomena Burnham mentions at various points in his essay: the recurrent vote of no-confidence for incumbent administrations; the large number of nonvoters; the decomposition of the Democratic party; the fragmentation of aggrieved constituencies into single-issue groups; the growing hostility within stable sections of the working class toward new claimant groups and insurgent movements; the declining proportions of young Americans who can hope to buy a home; the call from right and center for a shift from consumption to investment and from welfare to military expenditures; the rise of hedonism; the emergence of the Moral Majority. Each phenomenon on this list is a cause, a manifestation, or both, of disenchantment with the future available to our civilization.

It is true, of course, that the hedonist and the fundamentalist (as I shall call the convert to the Moral Majority) tend to diverge along lines of region, age, class, and urban/rural location. It is equally true that each holds the other in contempt, that the fundamentalist tends to migrate to the Republican party, and that the hedonists distribute themselves between the party of Democrats and the reserve army of nonvoters. But common threads of anxiety and sensibility run through these divisions. To draw out this common sense we must first revise one of the themes presented by Burnham.

The American state, says Burnham, is marked by a "constitution designed to fragment power" and "a culture which has a remarkably weak sense of collective public good." The first assessment is largely correct, though it can be argued that the American system visibly frag-

---

1. "The Eclipse of The Democratic Party," *Democracy* (July, 1982), pp. 7–17.

ments dissident constituencies while it invisibly encourages the coalescence of corporate hegemony through the dual media of the market and the state. It is the second assertion, though, that I wish to contest here. Burnham understates the degree to which the American people have shared a vision of the future and a sense of the common good. It is easy, perhaps, for intellectuals whose image of civic virtue and the common good is derived from a picture of the classical Greek polis to misread the common sensibility within American politics. For it contains the distinctive understanding that private initiative, self-reliance, and restricted state role provide both defining ingredients of the good life and essential preconditions of its realization.

Through much of the twentieth century, and certainly during the period from 1945 to 1963 discussed by Burnham, American political and social conflicts were at once diverse and contained within a widely shared vision of the good life in the making. This sense of the common good helped to set parameters to public conflicts, to establish the ground upon which compromises could be forged, and to justify (typically as temporary inconveniences) the uneven distribution of sacrifices and burdens borne within the country.

Two sets of priorities have governed our civilization. We have sought to perfect a private economy of growth and expanding affluence so that each generation could be more free, prosperous, and secure than the ones preceding it, and we have sought to sustain an inclusive political democracy flourishing within the confines of the American Constitution. Progress in America *meant* the growth of prosperity and the perfection of democratic rights. The legitimacy of the order, as we have known it, has revolved around the ability of each set of priorities to retain the allegiance of each new generation and the ability of each priority to progress in relative harmony with each other.

Now we are in a better position to interpret the historic break identified by Burnham. The pursuit of material progress for present and future generations now seems illusory to many, and the compatibility between that pursuit and democratic citizenship faces powerful strains. The phenomena that Burnham identifies as characteristic of America in the 1970s and 1980s represent symptoms of a massive withdrawal of sentiment from a comon vision of the future. The institutions that were to be the means of its realization have eroded the virtues of self-reliance and independence once thought to be essential to that vision. At the same time, there is growing anxiety about the future of economic growth and private affluence. As the credibility of the old economic dream recedes and as no new sense of a common future emerges to replace it, ordinary people create a variety of private strategies to secure

Civic Disaffection and the Democratic Party

a semblance of personal meaning and dignity in these new circumstances. Meanwhile elites strive to find new ways to impose new disciplines and limits on these ordinary people. We are thus witnessing the simultaneous emergence of an underground economy and an underground culture of civic disaffection in some circles and the introduction of new means of social control and ideological management of hope in others.

Hedonism and fundamentalism represent two instances of these defensive strategies. Each expresses, in its distinctive way, the declining credibility of the old American dream to new generations expecting to find meaning and significance in life. Hedonism is a withdrawal of sentiment from the larger life and an attempt to generate meaning from resources susceptible to one's own control. It thus concentrates on the pleasures of the body. Since the hedonist by definition repudiates civic virtue and the common good as restraints on pleasure, the only way to keep his conduct within the grooves demanded by private and public bureaucracies is to manipulate private desires and fantasies to serve public purposes. The rise of hedonism, in an order with highly developed imperatives of social coordination, impels state and private bureaucracies to devise finely tuned incentive systems and modes of coercive control.

Fundamentalism, expressed as rigid, punitive moralism authorized by personal experience of the word of God, constitutes a struggle to freeze the public world so that the future can be delayed. It is governed by fear of the future we are building. Private meaning is secured through the personal relation to God as the remoralized individual tries to insulate himself against the loss of significance in the larger life. But since the flow of the larger life now threatens to swamp this private morality it must be stilled. The punitive orientation to those who flout the revealed morality—for instance the hedonists—blocks the public flow of corrosive forces and suppresses dangerous ambiguities within the self concerning the restraints it endorses.

The retreat to pleasures of the self and to punitive moralism represent diverse responses to a common experience: the devaluation of the common good available in the social order. Until recently the sense of the common good was so widely shared there was little need to delineate its contours more closely through public debate. The debates centered on how to realize and protect it. But the element of commonality within which American conflicts and struggles have moved is burning out, even while a large cast of politicians and intellectuals tries heroically to rekindle the embers. Ends and standards we previously shared in common increasingly appear today as imperatives and burdens that th* order is compelled to impose if it is to sustain itself. The imperatives of capital accumulation and market protection require a shift from consumption to investment and from social to military expenditures; the number of people who can now expect to own a new home, provide higher education for their children, and sustain a fulfilling career is declining even though these represent paradigmatic components of the good life promised in America; items of consumption once experienced as luxuries to be enjoyed by one's children in the future now become necessities for participation in the life of the society; policies designed to protect the quality of air, water, and soil, and thereby to sustain the quality of human life for future generations, are dismantled because they pose obstacles to the expansion of private capital; old workers find themselves shunted to the sidelines in the name of perpetual economic progress, while their younger replacements glimpse the future for which *they* are being groomed; and the tightening web of international dependence, by multiplying points of apparent military insecurity, brings the civilization of productivity closer to its demise. The civilization of productivity—understood as those practices designed to promote economic growth and private affluence because they are thought to be good in themselves and essential preconditions to personal freedom and political democracy—finds itself pressed to subordinate all other ends to the interest of growth. The goal of the civilization of productivity becomes the imperative of growth.

In this context multiple strategies of withdrawal, evasion, and self-protection are not surprising. The surprise is that so few intellectuals read the symptoms correctly. As the ends of the civilization are increasingly experienced as imperatives, people define their lives accordingly. They prepare to resist and evade the disciplines applied to them or they join the growing cadres that invent and apply new controls to this recalcitrant material.

Are people today *simply* innocent of these conditions? Better to read the apparent innocence that persists in many quarters as a series of half-conscious strategies to ward off acknowledgment of the historical course we are on, to ward off, that is, the sense of disorientation which emerges when meaning and purpose are detached from the roles one is called upon to perform. Neoconservatives are apt to interpret the variety of life-styles, self-serving political demands, and underground strategies as immature or mindless refusals to accept lowered expectations. They are better comprehended, though, as fragile maneuvers to avoid becoming too mindful of clouds forming on the horizon of the civilization of productivity. We are in transition from a politics of the common good to a politics of system imperatives because we can now discern through historical experience the illusions inside our old dreams; and the experience of this transition, still unarticulated within the official terms of political discourse, permeates our institutional life.

The Role of the Welfare State

What parts do the state and, especially, the Democratic party play in these developments? The state is caught in a bind that sharply reduces its freedom to act creatively. Its range of options is limited because, on the one hand, it is supposed to be responsive to citizens through contested elections while, on the other, it is expected to support the system of private productivity by encouraging private capital accumulation and economic growth in an unfavorable environment. The needs and pleas of constituencies shuffled to the margins of the system of productivity are overridden by the need to establish a military shield for Western capitalism, by the play of domestic factions with impressive market and political resources, and by the pressure to eliminate those programs that weaken further the incentives to invest, the motivation to work, the sense of self-respect, and the willingness to abide by laws among those still incorporated within the life of the economy.

The welfare programs that result increase the dependence of beneficiaries, maintain them at low levels of support, demean them in their own eyes, and render them contemptible in the eyes of many clinging to modest roles and symbols of self-respect. The state faces a further limitation as well. It must not appear to socialize means of production while responding to the proliferating "side effects" of private enterprise. The experience of socialism in the twentieth century convinces Americans that the gap between socialist aspirations and achievements is even larger than that between the old American dream and its future prospects. Indeed the failure of covert symptoms of disengagement to coalesce into an insurgent political movement is linked to the common sense that the socialist alternative, as it has so far been articulated in theory and realized in practice, contains its own dialectic of social regimentation. The limited sense of alternatives encourages relatively well-positioned constituencies to endorse each new illusion defined by the right or center while it drives marginal elements to the underground economy and the class of nonvoters.

In these circumstances the Republican party may be able to define its mission with greater clarity, but it faces a series of credibility gaps as its appeals to the values of self-reliance and independence are mocked by measures that impose new dependencies and controls on the subordinate classes. Its willingness to give priority to imperatives emanating from the privately incorporated economy and to pressures flowing from western states now enjoying the expansionary run that precedes the emergence of urban malaise will shrink its share of the electorate after a period of incumbency. But it does attract a stable base of support; it does have a fairly clear agenda and a well-ordered battery of traditional symbols; and the party of nonvoters does provide it with a competitive edge.

The Democratic party faces a more volatile situation. Its natural base consists of a variety of state workers, scattered professionals, organized labor in the corporate sector, unorganized workers in the market sector, minorities facing discrimination, the marginally employed, the unemployed, and welfare recipients. But the programs it enacts to support the underclass pose threats to the identity available to many in the working class. When these tensions are accentuated the underclass loses the most because it has no other party to turn to. It tends to slide into the party of nonvoters under such conditions, while organized workers can threaten to defect to the Republican party or to sit out particular elections. The Democratic party is thus constrained in its quest to mobilize its largest potential coalition by the nature of two-party politics, the existing structure of electoral options, and the leverage available to organized elements of its coalition to forge compromises favoring them over the underclass. The Democratic party thus faces a dilemma rather than a range of alternatives: it can ignore the social needs of a large class of nonvoters, thereby perpetuating their powerlessness; or it can extend welfare state benefits to them, thereby alienating traditional Democratic supporters. Whichever way it turns it faces serious barriers to the creation of a stable coalition large enough to allow it to win office and govern effectively. And feeding this fragmentation of its coalition is not only the population shift to areas still relatively protected from the devastating effects of long-term corporate expansion but the fact that many residents in this virgin territory are refugees from areas previously serving as the prime targets of New Deal and Great Society programs. The potential Democratic coalition threatens to founder on the widely shared suspicion that four decades of welfare liberalism, promising to draw all Americans into the circle of affluence, freedom, and security, have increased dependence, demeaned the dignity of welfare recipients, and extended bureaucratic control into new spheres of American life. The welfare state is now considered by many a leviathan created by the Democratic party. That experience draws people into Republican rhetoric of reindustrialization, the creativity of free enterprise, and the personal ethic of self-reliance even while the operative programs of Nixon, Ford, and Reagan extend surveillance, militarize welfare, and restrict the life chances of a growing segment of the populace.

The dilemmas of the Democratic party cannot be ignored by dissidents who want to forge new forms of political organization that transcend conventional party politics. For the constitutional institution of elections through single-member districts and plurality vote means that an insurgent third party can aspire mainly to press the Democratic party to revise its priorities or, as a very long shot, to replace it as one of the two major parties. In either event, a new movement that succeeds will confront eventually the task of forging a viable coalition out of fragments that now elude the grasp of the Democratic party. Its chances of success will turn on its ability to speak to the civic disaffection generated during the period of hegemony by welfare liberalism.

Reconstituting Party Priorities

Is there a way out of this swamp? This question can be considered in sufficient depth and detail only through sustained dialogue by a diverse array of men and women who share enough to conclude that the accounts of reindustrialists, neoconservatives, and welfarists misconstrue our real condition and generate repressive implications. I believe that participants to this dialogue should consider (though certainly go beyond) the following agenda.

First, neither major party today speaks to the deep anxieties Americans feel about the prospects of thermonuclear war. Demands for effective arms control, for the demilitarization of American welfare, and for the deprofessionalization of American troops may alienate the military-industrial complex, but they will also draw creative constituencies into the party and release new energies within it. The construction of an affirmative electoral coalition could not achieve lasting monuments if it failed to roll back the militarization of American life and the probability of thermonuclear war.

Second, one of the major sources of welfare-state malaise resides in its imperative to support the continual expansion of corporate capital in the elusive effort to protect welfare benefits. A viable new movement must transcend the defensive posture welfare statists now adopt to those glowing with programs for economic growth and selective austerity. It must therefore devise ways to tame the growth imperative itself. If progress is not made on this front, the nation will shuffle back to the dismal options now before it. The debate over how to tame the growth imperative is yet to be opened. But one promising approach is to reduce the consumption needs of the populace by reconstituting irrational product forms that have become necessary objects of consumption in the American economy.[2] The forms of health care, transportation, housing, and food available in this country approach the status of exclusive goods: if restricted to the affluent they create hardships for the remaining populace that provides infrastructural support for these forms (for example, taxes to support complex medical training and technologies, highway systems, and air travel; tax deductions for mortgage interest; waste disposal and transportation subsidies for the food industry); if extended to the entire populace they damage the social and natural environment, increase social expenses borne by the state, and fuel inflationary wage demands by consumers scrambling to participate in the established universe of consumption. The constrant expansion of consumption needs generates much of the political support today for ruthless state policies to foster economic growth. There are more inclusive forms of health, transportation, housing, and food that could at once ease the demands on working-class budgets and draw the underclass more fully into the life of the society. These programs, if well designed, would drain electoral support for repressive strategies of reindustrialization and encourage constituencies now divided to draw closer together in a progressive political movement.

Third, the state must emphasize inclusive and universal programs over the selective and divisive programs it now presents. Some established welfare programs must be preserved, certainly, but new initiatives must move toward greater universality to establish justice in the distribution of state burdens and obligations and to draw old and new clients of the welfare state into a more cohesive constituency. The replacement of the professional army, now drawn from the underclass, by one recruited through a universal draft might be one step in the right direction; the universalization of military service might help to create more critical orientations to militarist policies and to provide the basis for the demilitarization of welfare. The inclusive modes of consumption

2. This is a large topic in need of further exploration. I have pursued it with Michael Best in *The Politicized Economy* (Lexington, Mass.: D.C. Heath, 1981). Two books that, taken together, explore the relations among consumption forms, the structure of social life, the pressures for growth, and the illusions of continued growth after a certain plateau has been attained are Mary Douglas and Baron Isherwood, *The World of Goods* (New York: Basic Books, 1979), and Fred Hirsch, *The Social Limits to Growth* (Cambridge, Mass.: Harvard University Press, 1977).

Civic Disaffection and the Democratic Party

referred to above would be consistent with this principle as well. Family allowances would help to maintain the integrity of family life without encouraging some workers to believe that their families are taxed to keep nonworking families intact.

Fourth, while continuing to dramatize the dangers, dependencies, divisions, and injustices built into reindustrialization scenarios of the right and center, a new movement, which hopes to be as pertinent in our day as the New Deal was in its, will express renewed appreciation for the values of self-respect, self-reliance, and local initiative. The hegemony of the liberal welfare state during the four decades has allowed the right to capture rhetorical control of these symbols even while programs of the right strip people of the skills, resources, and dignity they need to live according to these standards.

There are several areas in which space for self-reliance might be established while claims of equity and justice were supported, including: the production of durable commodities simple enough in design to allow owners to repair them; the introduction of energy forms centered in the home or locality rather than controlled by policies of corporate giants; state policies that encourage families to flourish as stable units; the reconstruction of a transportation system, now organized around the automobile, to allow urban residents, the disabled, the poor, and the elderly to reestablish mobility; the reintroduction of childbirth in the home; and the legalization of many barter agreements now officially defined to fall within the underground economy. Each of the proposals needs to be considered in detail before it is endorsed, but the point in listing them here is to illustrate how the values of self-reliance and justice might be supported by state initiatives that transcend the primacy of market power and corporate priorities.

Consider, in the same spirit, how a reconstitution of the American health care system could foster three of the standards elucidated above. Medical care in America is structured by the capacity of physicians to set fees privately; a partially collectivized system of payments; high technology; curative treatment; and the proliferation of malpractice suits initiated by maltreated patients. It is an irrational system, which must either exclude many or become inclusive by feeding inflation and civic disaffection. And the state is heavily invested in it. In 1981 the state lost between $17.5 and $24 billion in potential tax revenues on health insurance premiums and $3.4 billion in individual medical deductions. Current state policy magnifies the power of physicians over patients by partially collectivizing payments and leaving power to set fees in private hands, while its own subsidies favor the affluent over the poor. When total state medical subsidies are considered, 45 percent reach poor and low-income people while 55 percent go to the affluent.[3] A rational policy would divert much of the $35 billion in total state funds supporting the current health care system to one embodying local, prepaid health care centers, salaried medical and paramedical staff accountable to its members, an emphasis on preventive over curative care, and the return of a large portion of health knowledge, skills, and responsibilities to individuals and families. As successful experiments with such a design already show, its system of rewards and accountability encourages physicians to promote greater patient self-sufficiency in health care; to concentrate on maintaining an individual's health over the entire course of his or her life; and to control patients' costs through salaries rather than fees, a lower rate of surgery, and more preventive care. Such a design contains the potential for extension to the entire populace without contributing to new rounds of inflation, political resentment, and medical corruption. It is an *inclusive* good that also fosters self-reliance.

A new democratic movement on the left must advance on three fronts at once. It must seek to revitalize the relation between the state and the citizen, to tame imperatives flowing from the privately incorporated economy, and to establish new economic priorities that allow all members of the society to be full-fledged citizens. To advance on any of these fronts it must make comparable progress on the others. Liberals and Democrats who fail to follow this course will find themselves drawn increasingly into the orbit of right-wing strategies of reindustrialization, selective austerity, and disciplinary control—all endorsed in the name of economic rationality.

3. These figures are taken from a study of Gail Wilensky for the Center for Health Services Research as reported in the *New York Times,* January 1, 1981.

4 PROGRESS, GROWTH, AND

PESSIMISM IN AMERICA

The Present and the Future

To be human is to live in the shadow of the future, to have one's thoughts, moods, and actions touched by one's understanding of prospects and possibilities. To be a people, sharing or contesting a way of life, is to invest current practices and standards with a sense of the collective future they foster.

The bearing of the future on the present is clear enough in the life of the individual. Insurance payments serve as a hedge against future losses; a student's academic program is informed by career prospects; anxiety is triggered by contemplation of one's unavoidable death. But the relation between perceptions of the future prospects of an entire civilization and the shape of current social practices may appear less immediate or powerful. Can one not, for instance, shield oneself from collective hardships or disasters looming on the horizon? One can try at least. And the collective impact of a series of such defensive strategies helps to determine the tenor of life in the present.

Even in an individualist culture the current life of the self is intimately bound up with its perception of the future fate of the collectivity, and the fate of the collectivity is joined to participant perception of its probable future. Consider one dimension of this relationship. To face the inevitability of one's death is to discern that one's transactions in family, work, education, and politics touch others and the future as much as they do oneself now. One leaves monuments to the living upon one's death, bestowing the legacy of one's efforts as a parent, worker, teacher, and citizen.

This connection between the life of the self and the fate of the collectivity, mediated by our morality, enters silently into the performances of those who appreciate the common future they are building. But when the future becomes devalued or depreciated by the present—perhaps because its highest prospects now ring hollow or because the future of current or past achievements appears dim—the common life in the present changes too. When mortals doubt the value of the legacy they can bestow upon the future, the job performance, investment strategies, tax payment practices, gender relations, child rearing, and political orientations of the living tend to deteriorate. The claims of immediacy and self assume priority over those of the future and the common life. And when such a shift occurs, the common life is modified profoundly even while its formal institutional structure may remain intact.

America has been built around the promise of extending freedom, justice, and rights to the entire populace, where freedom is defined as independence from external domination, especially at the hands of the state; rights are viewed as trump cards to be played whenever public or private authorities fail to respect the dignity of the person; and justice means the provision of equal opportunity to achieve a good livelihood and to live a prosperous life. These ideals in turn are tied first, to the idea of a constitutional democracy that renders the government accountable to its citizenry, and second, to a privately incorporated economy that realizes these hopes progressively through the generation of economic growth and the insulation of economic relations from undue state intrusion. The expectation of economic growth is now so closely linked to the established understandings of freedom, dignity, and justice that the threat of persistent economic stagnation poses a threat to every other end of the civilization. If the future means progress then it must also mean a steady rate of economic expansion. That is the assumption of the American creed and the presupposition of its political economy.

But if growth has been the hinge upon which the American future turns, the future now appears gloomy. Does anyone believe that we can maintain during the next fifty years anything like the growth rate secured during the past fifty? Whichever way we turn it appears that obstacles to future growth will be overwhelming or that its realization will be at the expense of ends that have traditionally justified it. A more rational policy of investment? Then (it is said) we must insulate the political process from irrational public pressures, and we must curtail consumption to expand investment. A more productive work force? We must subject workers to new disciplines, preferably through a "new social contract," but by other means if necessary. A shift from "sunset" to "sunrise" industries? We must press workers in the frost belt to pull up stakes again (many emigrated from the South just a couple of generations ago), and move away from the family and community ties that now give a degree of protection from the vicissitudes of the economy. Too many people who are inessential to or disruptive of the growth process? They must be neutralized. An increase in corruption and crime on the job? Increase the scope and size of private security forces. Welfare costs that drain the economy? We must militarize welfare by shifting the unruly elements out of the civilian sector, and we must improve the monitoring capacity of civilian agencies that deal with the remaining clients.

At every turn barriers to growth become occasions to tighten social control, to build new hedges around citizen rights, to insulate bureaucracies from popular pressures while opening them to corporate influence, to rationalize work processes, to impose austerity on vulnerable constituencies, to delay programs for environmental safety, to legitimize military adventures abroad. Growth, previously seen as the means to realization of the good life, has become a system imperative to which elements of the good life are sacrificed. We thus lose both if growth is realized and if it is not. The very link between the American idea of progress and the imperative of economic growth today fosters a profound and pervasive mood of pessimism in American life.

This pessimism can be detected in many currents of American culture, in reactions that simultaneously express disaffection from system imperatives, disrupt efforts to meet those imperatives, and foster public and private strategies to bring the disaffected back into line. The burgeoning underground economy manifests, among other things, the view that the existing tax system is unfair and the current shape of public expenditures is ill designed to serve those stuck in the lower reaches of the economy. The erosion of family life, the rising divorce rate, and gender struggles contain the perception that traditional modes of sacrifice are unlikely to generate secure future for the next generation. The rise of the litigious personality signifies a growing strain of belligerence in asserting the claims of self against those of the common life. The rise of creationism and hedonism, as described above, reflects a common anxiety about the future we are preparing and our powerlessness to reshape it. They represent extreme manifestations of a glacial shift in our public life and private sensibilities.

Why are these symptoms, with the exception of elements in the antinuclear, ecology, and feminist movements, not more overtly expressed in our current political discourse? What does the strain of pessimism that pervades public discourse reveal about it and our condition?

One theme cuts across the disparate positions formulated by those who seek to comprehend and improve America during the last fifth of the twentieth century. Commentators on the right, left, and center generally concur in giving primacy to economic growth. With enthusiasm or reluctance, through affirmation or evasion, they sanction a variety of actions that sacrifice some ingredients in the American ideal of democracy to the current imperative of growth.

On the right George Gilder, eulogizing the creativity of capitalist growth, calls for a respiritualization of America to reinvigorate the economy. This economization of spirituality rests upon the view that "faith in man, faith in the future, faith in the rising return of giving, faith in the mutual benefits of trade, faith in the providence of God are all essential to successful capitalism."[1] Gilder discerns the inner relation between the health of an order and its members' confidence in the future it prepares, but the stridency of his recipe for respiritualization reveals how thoroughly it flies in the face of our lived relation to the future. Such spiritual reinvigoration would today have to be imposed; the Protestant ethic cannot rekindle itself, party because the future it once dreamed is too much at odds with the one we now discern.

Sensing this, Gilder offers a variety of proposals to induce changes in behavior wherever his evangelical message fails to spawn spirituality. His text consists of a series of state strategies to release corporations from state control while subjecting the working poor, welfare recipients, workers in sunset industries, public employees, frost-belt communities, minorities, and women to a variety of new controls and economic austerity.

Samuel Huntington, in his recent book *The Promise of Disharmony,* sponsors a more subdued and secular version of the Gilder thesis.[2] The "American Creed," as he thoughtfully formulates its character and history, celebrates constitutionalism, freedom, equality, and decentralization. But institutional imperatives, lodged in the very structure of modernity, require inequality, bureaucratization, economic growth, a centralized state, and a strong military presence in the world. Recurrent periods of "creedal passion," periods when dissident forces crystallize around the demand to bring institutions into line with ideals, are thus dangerously ambiguous phenomena. They embody much that is admirable and distinctive about America, but their success would undermine the institutional conditions for expression of the creed. There is a dilemma here that we must learn to live with.

There are admirable points in Huntington's elucidation of our condition, but the frame in which it is enunciated guarantees which side must give way whenever the latent dilemma becomes overt. The artificial separation of institutions and ideals bestows reality and solidity on the former and dependence and plasticity on the latter. One exists in the world; the other in our heads. So when institutional demands and democratic ideals conflict sharply the latter must always adjust to the former. The promise of disharmony is the promise of maintaining tension

1. *Wealth and Poverty* (New York: Basic Books, 1980).
2. Cambridge: Harvard University Press, 1981.

Progress, Growth, and Pessimism in America

between the two as long as it is clear which side receives hegemony. As Hungtington puts it, "an increasingly sophisticated economy and active involvement in world affairs seems likely to create stronger needs for hierarchy, bureaucracy, centralization of power, expertise, big government. . . . In some way or another, society will respond to these needs while still attempting to realize the values of the American creed to which they are so contradictory." The distribution of emphasis places "needs" on one side and "values" on the other; the institutions "create" needs; we "attempt" to preserve ideals.

Huntington, unlike Gilder, recognizes that the imperative of growth entails new burdens and sacrifices to creedal values, and though he is ready to tolerate what it takes to face up to this reality, he is rather pessimistic about the prospects for doing so. The American creed, once standing in a relation of creative tension with institutional demands, has now become more of an obstacle to their realization. The sixties and seventies fostered the erosion of authority by exposing its misuses. "The American political system, which is so superbly designed to prevent and to rectify abuses of authority," Hungtington says, "is very poorly equipped to reverse the erosion of authority." The sixties left America with severe "foreign and domestic challenges that required the exercise of power yet still unwilling to legitimize power." Imperatives lodged in our institutions, and ideals lodged in our heads, make Huntington pessimistic about the future while preparing him to endorse whatever it takes to adjust to those imperatives.

The Politics of Bifurcation

Things become more complex when we turn to the drift of contemporary liberalism. Here a bifurcation has emerged with one side devoting itself to technical agendas to foster growth and discipline and the other retreating to an abstract celebration of liberal ideals. The bifurcation of liberals into technocrats and beautiful souls reflects the inability of liberalism today to sponsor a coherent doctrine that ties the ideals of freedom, justice, and rights to a specific institutional context capable of securing them for the future. (See also below, Chap. 6.)

Thus Lester Thurow, perhaps the leading candidate for chief economic adviser in the next Democratic administration, calls for significant changes in our economic and political institutions.[3] Each of these changes is designed to remove impediments to, or create incentives for,

3. *The Zero-Sum Society* (New York: Basic Books, 1980).

new growth spirals: "Current productivity growth rates are deeply embedded in the structure of our economy and major changes would be necessary before we see major improvement." Thurow blames the porous character of the political process for failure to adopt rational growth policies. America's success in "the modern growth race" depends on its ability to convert the political process into a system for managing the economy and distributing the costs of change rationally. Thurow's text consists mostly of technical solutions to the problem of growth; and his treatment of education, gender, and other social relations testifies how far the economization of politics has proceeded in technocratic liberalism. But Thurow is nonetheless pessimistic about the political prospects for reform, and his pessimism has its source in an understanding of the American creed that resembles that of Huntington. Our politics is unsusceptible to economic rationality. This realization eventually authorizes a somber mood at odds with the optimistic glow emanating from his technical recipes for growth.

> Will we fail as a society to address the fundamental problem and let it drag us down with it? Perhaps. In the record of history, we certainly would not be the first society that failed to come to grips with its fundamental internal problems.

While technocrats shuffle liberal ideals into the background to concentrate on growth scenarios, another constellation of liberals gives primacy to the ideals by detaching discussion of them from the institutional imperatives of the order. The attraction of liberalism has been its promise to join liberal principles to practical courses of action capable of gaining assent in the short term. But the beautiful souls of contemporary liberalism recall their Hegelian ancestors by enunciating ideals in detail, by holding public authority responsible for fulfilling them, and by refusing to confront structural characteristics of the political economy that threaten them. The beautiful soul "lives in dread of besmirching the splendour of its inner being by action . . . in order to preserve the purity of its heart . . . it flees from contact with the actual world and persists in its self-willed impotence to give itself a substantial existence or to translate its thought into being."[4]

---

4. G.W.F. Hegel, *The Phenomenology of Spirit*, trans. A.V. Miller (Oxford: Clarendon Press, 1977), pp. 399–400. I choose these critical terms to characterize this stance partly because I feel drawn to it despite its defects. There are circumstances, indeed, where it is the most rational and moral stance to adopt. Where the world is thoroughly at odds with authentic principles, such a stance can keep the idea alive. But the beautiful soul protects the appearance of purity by cultivating innocence about the historical course of the world. Its quest for purity overwhelms its ability to confront the actual way of the world.

John Rawls's *A Theory of Justice* exemplifies this mode nicely.[5] The text adumbrates a set of standards against which existing economic and political arrangements are to be assessed, but it draws a veil of ignorance across the institutional arrangements to which the standards apply. The text is abstract not only in its formulation of standards but in its characterization of the institutional world in which those standards are to be realized. It opposes the utilitarianism of technocratic liberals but does not comprehend how the political economy it endorses generates the utilitarian mode. It retains a liberal guise by ignoring major institutional reforms necesary to withstand the operative hegemony of utilitarianism. Its quest for purity encourages it to float above the world it judges, and hence its frustratingly abstract and vague mode of presentation vitiates the power of its moral message. It puts "judging . . . above the deeds it discredits, wanting its words without deeds to be taken for a superior kind of reality."[6] Rawls's abstract style is thus not an incidental flaw in an otherwise solid theory; it is today the necessary medium for the purity he seeks to preserve.

A more recent and ambiguous instance is Michael Walzer's *Spheres of Justice.*[7] This text persuasively challenges the abstract universalism of Rawls; it sensitively draws out the complex standards of justice built into the American way of life, showing why we demarcate different spheres of justice in the areas of welfare, office holding, work assignment, leisure, and education. Because it is more specific and persuasive than the Rawlsian position it opposes, it teaches us much about the complex inner rationale of norms implicitly endorsed in our practices.

But at another level Walzer's text recapitulates the Rawlsian stance. Walzer convinces us, for example, that "a decent state . . . will act to maintain the integrity of its various institutional settings: to make sure that its prisons are places for criminal internment and not for preventive detention or scientific experiment; that its schools are not like prisons; that its asylums house (and care for) the mentally ill and not the politically deviant." But these and other standards are stated as if the moral will to protect them in the current setting suffices to guarantee their protection. Walzer's opposition to technocratic controls is sustained by putting distance between his standards and practices repugnant to them, not by showing how the latter are avoidable within the economic priorities he endorses.

Why is this tendency so strongly developed in liberalism today?

5. Cambridge: Harvard University Press, 1971.
6. Hegel, *Phenomenology,* p. 405.
7. New York: Basic Books, 1983.

Because, I suggest, the tension between the imperatives of the contemporary welfare state and the ideals of liberalism are becoming too intense to defend both in detail within the confines of one text. There *is* something honorable in a stance that innocently affirms these ideals in difficult circumstances. It keeps appreciation of the ideals alive and sets limits of tolerance to technocratic intrusions. But there is a corollary danger in this defensive strategy as well: it precludes creative reconsideration of the future prospects generated by current practices and exploration of ways to reconstitute the practices so that those prospects look better.

Liberal technocrats shuffle liberal principles into a corner in pursuit of practicality, and liberal idealists express their ideals beautifully by avoiding practicality. When the two sides of bifurcated liberalism are considered together they can be seen to be alternative evasions of the same condition: since the growth imperative of the political economy of private productivity is increasingly at odds with liberal principles that legitimize the end of growth, the soulful liberal retreats to the abstract "ought" to evade complicity in harsh scenarios of growth while the soulless liberal constructs growth scenarios that would stifle liberal ideals.

The contemporary left tends to recapitulate a radical variant of liberal bifurcation. Marxists, usually trained as economists, try to convince us that a well-ordered socialist society will foster growth, community, and justice together. But defections from this version of radicalism are legion; many radicals have shifted to an emphasis on localism and participatory modes spiced with a touch of anarchism. This latter stance is exemplified in the work of Michel Foucault, whose thought has now become part of the currency of the American left.

Foucault's theory of "disciplinary society" is illuminating because it examines microstructures of power lodged within existing forms of sexuality, delinquency, architectural design, insanity, and medicine in ways that challenge the established understandings of radicals and liberals. Foucault treats contemporary ideals of socialism, for instance, as idealistic intensifications of disciplinary society. Radical socialists must give up the rhetorical style of "inverted commas," whereby they protect the true ideal of socialism by differentiating it thoroughly from every existing order that now calls itself socialist. The "only socialism which deserves these scornful scare quotes is the one which leads the dreamy life of ideality in our heads."[8]

Foucault, by releasing us from the obligation to endorse any existing

8. *Power and Knowledge* (New York: Pantheon Books, 1981).

or ideal order, unleashes critical impulses previously constrained by the obligation to endorse one or another set of constraints in modernity. In distancing ourselves from all forms of established discipline we are better able to discern or experience forms of subjugation built into the microstructures of social life; we are thereby encouraged to treat every *limit* as an *imposition*. Foucault thus can commend tactics that move below the level of the state. Eschewing electoral politics and national movements aimed at changing state priorities, he calls for the proliferation of "local, specific, struggles" at those numerous junctures where bureaucratic power impinges upon client populations. "The role for theory today seems to me to be just this: not to formulate the global systematic theory which holds everything in place, but to analyze the specificity of mechanisms of power, to locate the connections and extensions, to build little by little a strategic knowledge." These local, dispersed tactics of resistance avoid drawing participants into the orbit of state control or into the sticky web of counterideals.

Foucault symbolizes a variety of tendencies on the contemporary left. Even though the theory illuminates some dark corners of modernity,[9] the general attraction to its strategic orientation is a sympton of retreat and despair on the left. We have here the beautiful soul in radical disguise.

There is a dilemma of radical change that grips the modern state and helps to explain both the bifurcation of contemporary liberalism and the magnetic power of Foucauldian politics for the contemporary left. The parameters of this dilemma were exposed dramatically during the May 1968 revolt in France and have surfaced several times since, most recently and modestly during the Tylenol episode of 1982 in the United States. Such events reveal a duality inscribed in modern institutional life. First, authority and effective power are fragile; they are vulnerable to periodic disruptions and disturbances because of the intricate institutional interdependencies that mark modernity. The smooth operation of the order can be disrupted or stymied at certain moments by a determined, militant faction or movement. As the Tylenol episode illustrated in microcosm, the entire distribution network that moves essential goods and services from points of production to point of consumption is highly vulnerable to disruption. The network of interdependencies creates multiple possibilities for disturbance and subversion; it is the existence of such levers that gives the aura of credibility to Foucauldian tactics.

9. See Chaps. 7, 8, and 10, below.

But, second, each occasion of localized disruption tends eventually to strengthen the mechanisms of order, surveillance, and intimidation at the previous locus of attack. Airline hijacking, cyanide poisoning of consumer products, attacks on the military presence in university life, and the popular revolt in Poland constitute superb examples of this phenomenon. Why is this? Some analysts postulate a craving for authority that haunts even those who engage in disruption. But it seems to me that the very phenomenon that creates opportunities for disruption also generates the reactive pressures for militant restoration. The web of interdependencies into which we are drawn makes it difficult or impossible for people to prove self-sufficient when existing institutions are disrupted severely. The network of interdependencies thereby spawns political support for normalization after a period of disruption. The nostalgia for self-reliance in contemporary America is thus not merely an excuse by the right to ignore the needs of dependent constituencies; it also involves a more pervasive yearning for a world in which it is possible to express contempt for existing rules and institutions by retreating to an enclave of self-subsistence. This yearning for independence finds expression in the individualism of the right and the enclave communalism of the left.

This combination of fragile power and self-regenerating power is built into the institutional matrix of modern life, and when the combination itself is acknowledged, defects in regional strategies of resistance become transparent. It becomes clear that localism and radical resistance cannot suffice in a world where the state is intertwined in the details of life and the focal point of imperatives facing the political economy as a whole. The duality also exposes the moment of truth in conservative capitulation to those imperatives. The imperatives must either be accepted or subjected to attack at the level of the state. They cannot be ignored or defined out of existence.

Liberals and radicals today must seek to enhance the space for democratic politics through generation of state action that relaxes or tames the imperative of economic growth. Such a strategy requires, first, a thorough reassessment of the historical connections between the American idea of progress and the goal of constant economic expansion and, second, the identification of those institutional forces that simultaneously generate the growth imperative and political support for it. For when the present lives at the expense of the future it also lives at the expense of the present.

5 THE CRITICAL THEORY

OF JÜRGEN HABERMAS

The Scope of Critical Theory

Every contemporary social theorist must eventually confront the thought of Jürgen Habermas. One may be interested in a critique of positivism, in probing the limits of instrumental rationality, in exploring the relations between theory and practice, in comprehending the intersubjective dimension of social life and the hermeneutic mode of apprehending it, in ascertaining how an intersubjectively constituted social world could become mired in structural constraints, in connecting the psychoanalytic dialogue to the project of social critique, in establishing linkages between the logic of personal development and the logic of social legitimation, in penetrating the sources of the legitimacy deficit facing advanced capitalist systems, in revising the Marxian account of capitalism to fit the conditions of political economy in the late twentieth century, or in establishing an epistemological basis for social critique and legitimation. If one is interested in any of these issues—more important, if one is concerned with how conclusions reached in each of these domains limit and enable judgment in the others—then one will eventually delve into the studies launched by Habermas over the past twenty years.

Habermas can exasperate theorists in the Anglo-American tradition. While we tend to concentrate on one or two issues at a time, hoping that clarity in one area wil provide firm foundations for solid construction in others, the thought of Habermas is unconfined by temporal or disciplinary boundaries. The very range of his thought seem to ensure that it will be thin and undisciplined, and specialists in each area do undoubtedly find much to criticize. But the mode of speculative theory Habermas practices generates a form of discipline unavailable to more insulated inquiries. In a speculative theory, claims articulated in one domain can be checked for their consistency, or, more permissively, consonance, with assumptions accepted in others. Judgments reached with confidence in one area can be brought to bear on issues posed in more problematic or mysterious areas of a theory. And, since every specialized theory necessarily draws upon uninvestigated assumptions in a variety of allied fields, one could argue that speculative theory, when it is done well, provides more clarity and discipline than theory of the more restrained sort. The more encompassing the theory, the greater the variety of coherence tests each of the component parts must pass. The Habermas project, pursued in the classic tradition of social theory, thus provides an invaluable touchstone against which presuppositions implicitly embedded in more limited theories can be identified and assessed.

The drawbacks to speculative theory are clearly discernible to us today. Few people are capable of mastering the multiple fields of discourse essential to such an enterprise; fewer yet are able to bring the resources of one field, bounded by its specialized vocabulary and instrumentalities, within the horizon of alternative fields. Certainly, Jürgen Habermas must be accorded high marks for his efforts, given the level of difficulty generated by the contemporary proliferation of disciplines. He has penetrated a number of fields, if seldom to the complete satisfaction of those specializing in them, and often he has found ways to open dialogue where previously communication had been frozen. The debates with Popper, Gadamer, and Lühmann, the exchanges with Anglo-American philosophers indebted to Wittgenstein and Austin, radical American political economists, and theorists of moral development testify to that achievement. The exchange typically begins with the specialists (though some of these thinkers range fairly widely themselves) complaining about certain misunderstandings on the part of Habermas and end by many of those ranged on each side viewing their own enterprise in a more refined way.

The texts translated to date, thanks in part to Thomas McCarthy, provide Anglo-American social theorists an opportunity to reassess selective presuppositions in their own thought. And McCarthy's *Critical Theory of Jürgen Habermas,*[1] thorough in its coverage and alert to the bearing of Habermas' thought on a variety of Anglo-American schools, allows us to take the measure of the entire Habermasian project as it has evolved to date. McCarthy has drawn these diverse materials together beautifully, sifting through the central arguments at each stage of Habermas' development and revealing the relation that each part bears to the larger project. McCarthy's exegesis is always lucid and fair; his identification of gaps and defects in the arguments is usually perspicuous. His account, I think, is strongest in its exposition of the critique of instrumental reason, the relations between critical theory and hermeneutics and the evolving theory of communication competence.

1. Cambridge, Mass.: MIT Press, 1978. Further citations are in the text.

The Critical Theory of Jürgen Habermas

In these chapters McCarthy mediates effectively between the traditions of discourse within which Habermas moves and the contours of our own thought. McCarthy's accounts of the critique of psychoanalysis, the reconstruction of dialectical materialism, and the theory of legitimacy crisis in advanced capitalism are also illuminating. But his own voice recedes into the background in these chapters. He seldom defends, challenges, or clarifies the voice of Habermas. It is perhaps too much to expect otherwise; for in the chapters in which he brings the resources of alternative traditions of discourse to bear on one another, he sets a standard which would be impossible to maintain throughout the text.

McCarthy criticizes some of the formulations in Habermas' early text *Knowledge and Human Interests*. After presenting Habermas' three cognitive interests, namely the technical, the communicative, and the emancipatory interests, McCarthy questions Habermas' tendency to link each cognitive interest to a particular social practice. To reduce, for instance, our cognitive relation to nature to an interest in bringing it under technical control is too restrictive.

> Are we not left in the end with only one legitimate attitude toward nature: technical mastery? And is this not seriously inadequate as an account of the multi-faceted relationships with nature, both "outer nature" and the "inner nature" of our own bodies . . . ? Habermas does not exclude the possibility of other *attitudes* toward nature—mimetic, poetic, playful, mystical, fraternal. . . . But his theory does seem to exclude modes of cognizing nature other than empirical-analytic. . . . On what grounds could all cognitive content be denied to those modes of consciousness described above as attitudes . . . ? (67)

And McCarthy raises further questions about the arguments in *Knowledge and Human Interests*. He contends that the emancipatory interest, the interest in those processes of self-reflection which free the subject from unnecessary and unjustified constraints, cannot be placed on a par with the interests in technical control and communicative interaction. It is parasitic upon the two fundamental spheres of "work and interaction"; for they provide the sites within which emancipatory efforts are situated and the materials from which the quest for emancipation is constructed. McCarthy also contends that Habermas, in tendency at least, conflates two separable aspects of emancipation—a reflective process through which illegitimate restrictions implicit in established norms are exposed and a process of practical engagement through which we strive to reconstitute those restrictive practices. The conflation, if it were consistently adopted, would support a set of political illusions associated with the tradition of philosophical idealism; it therefore cuts against the grain of Habermasian thought in other domains.

McCarthy worries too about a tendency in Habermasian thought to deflate the distinction between reflection upon the transcendental conditions of knowledge and freedom and reflection upon the specific conceptions of self and society presupposed by participants within a particular way of life; for arguments developed at the first level cannot provide a sufficient basis for the critique of those ideologies embedded in particular ways of life. McCarthy points out, as well, that in his most recent work Habermas has himself acknowledged the importance of this distinction.

Finally, McCarthy contends that the Habermas of these early essays is plagued by the same dilemma which gripped earlier versions of critical theory—namely: if critical theory points to systematic distortions in participant self-understandings within contemporary society, it must acknowledge standards against which the distortion is measured; but if the distortion is thought to be too systematic, then critical theory must be treated as another symptom of the disease it seeks to diagnose. Habermas was alert to the dilemma as it found expression in earlier versions of critical theory, and he aspired to dissolve it. But McCarthy feels impelled to raise similar questions about *Knowledge and Human Interests.* "To what standard does this materialist phenomenology appeal in unmasking ideological world views and forms of life? To what perception or theory of reality does it appeal in characterizing other preceptions and theories as distorted? To what theory of history does it appeal in distinguishing progressive from regressive modes of thought and practice?" (108)

Habermas, in his later work, seeks to locate the needed standards inside the structure of human communication. The widespread wariness with which this project has been greeted is readily understandable. For in examining the presuppositions of a way of life it seems always debatable whether the unnecessary has been filtered from the necessary and the particular from the universal; or whether, instead, certain particularities which express the deep-seated hopes and prejudices of an era or of a faction have been universalized illicitly. Habermas' reply, signified by the persistence with which he pursues this project, seems unassailable to me. The project—though not perhaps his own fulfillment of it—is both extremely problematic and inherently unavoidable for anyone who engages in social critique and justification. Those who believe the enterprise is unnecessary eventually find it necessary to articulate to others the rationale implicit in the tradition (or "prejudice") to which they appeal; and those who would deflate the aspiration to universality within this enterprise imply that they have rational grounds for doing so. In criticizing specific formulations by Habermas such theorists are inadvertently drawn into the orbit of his larger project.

Habermas' explorations of psychoanalysis and hermeneutics are informed by this quest to formulate rational standards of critique; his theory of communication is an effort to consolidate insights drawn from these traditions, and from other traditions as well, into a coherent theory or rational discourse; and his interpretation of tendencies in late capitalism to generate standards of legitimation that the system itself cannot live up to constitutes a concrete application of the evolving theory of communication. I will examine each of these inquiries briefly, drawing sustenance from McCarthy's commentary.

Critical Theory and Psychoanalysis

Both Freud and Habermas believe that self-conscious awareness of the deep background of conduct and relationships can contribute to the greater coherence and realism of future action. But the necessity of stating the affinity between them in such extremely general terms reveals how deep the differences cut. Freud doubted in principle the ability of the subject to bring all ingredients of the unconscious to the level of conscious understanding and control, while Habermas has not identified any *necessary* set of limits to the self-transparency of the subject; Freud shied away from the pursuit of collective self-consciousness, yet that pursuit is both intrinsically important and a precondition of personal self-consciousness for Habermas; Freud did not formulate a refined theory of intersubjectivity—of the ways in which subjects are constituted by a background set of socially established concepts, beliefs, and aspirations—while the theory of intersubjectivity figures prominently in the work of Habermas; Freudian therapy tends to reconcile patients to the established system (though there are of course exceptions), while such advice must often be viewed by Habermas as part of the larger disease to be exposed; the theory-evidence relation in Freudian theory is based largely upon the doctor-patient couple within an established social order, while that nexus in Habermasian theory is anchored in a more global comparison of societal types.

Given such discrepancies in basis and mission, it is easy to expect extrapolations in either direction to be filled with mutual misunderstanding. McCarthy notes, for instance, that the analogy drawn by Habermas between the critique of ideology and the therapeutic session breaks down if pushed too literally. What position, he asks, is the critical theorist placed in if "he has not only to inform oppressed groups of their ideological self-deception but also to overcome their 'resistance'?" And, "if he has to do this not only outside of but in opposition to sustaining authority, what are his chances of success? Of survival?" (212) The danger of a slide into a manipulative relationship, serious enough in the psychoanalytic dialogue where the psychoanalyst expects transference, resistance, and regression on the part of the patient, is exacerbated profoundly when the therapist-patient model is translated into a model for political emancipation.

But Habermas, as McCarthy himself suspects, does not seem to take the psychoanalytic model so literally. To do so would be to depoliticize relationships which participants already comprehend insufficiently through political categories. Judgments concerning the necessity or desirability of such apolitical relationships depend upon a prior judgment of how severely unconscious controls must in principle inhibit the very possibility of an informed, democratic politics in modern life.

We can clarify this latent disparity in orientation by considering the recent criticism by Donald McIntosh of Habermas' interpretation of Freudian theory. Habermas, McIntosh contends, wants both to save the Kantian idea of the subject and to draw upon the insights of Freudian theory. But he cannot have it both ways. For Freud's theory of the unconscious places stringent limits on the subject's ability to achieve self-consciousness, and these limits are essential both to the psychic economy of the individual and to the maintenance of social civility. "Of course it would be nice to have a society where people had strong enough egos to hold such (aggressive) impulses in check consciously, without undue anxiety. But this is fantasy. On both the social and psychological levels internalized unconscious controls are necessary."[2] Habermas does not deny the *possibility* that this thesis is true, though he thinks we are not today in a position to ascertain just how extensive such controls must be in a well-ordered society. Habermas' reading of Freud, I believe, is not so much a misreading as a selective reading designed to preserve certain Freudian insights without, implicitly or explicitly, repudiating the very idea of a subject who is capable of deliberately shaping conduct to rules, of appreciating the significance of action for others, of exercising self-restraint, and of reflexively reconstituting old habits to promote new purposes.

2. "Habermas on Freud," *Social Research* 44 (1977):596.

There is an unresolved tension in Freudian theory between an intentionalist view of the subject and structural theory of the unconscious. Certain readings of the theory of the unconscious license a restrictive view of the subject who is potentially able to translate some of the unconscious into conscious ideas, to reassess those ideas by reference to argument and evidence, and to form future intentions on the basis of these new assessments. Other, more strigent, readings submerge the idea of the subject Habermas seeks to preserve and enhance.

The systematic (or structural) theory treats the unconscious as an internally integrated structure, following laws of its own. Mental processes, incorporated into this system, exhibit a set of characteristics which differentiate them radically from conscious processes. Richard Wollheim, surely the leading philosophical interpreter of Freud in the Anglo-American world, identifies these characteristics succinctly: "exemption from mutual contradiction, primary process, timelessness, and replacement of external by internal reality."[3] Such a theory severs the very relation between conscious and unconscious processes. How could any idea or wish, once shuffled into this system, remain determinate enough to be readmissible in principle to consciousness? And how could unconscious processes, so structured, exert determinate effects on the conscious emotional life? Any version of Freudian therapy which seeks to raise the patient's "soft voice of reason" to a higher pitch (not all forms do) cannot consistently maintain such a highly structured theory of the unconscious. It certainly cannot be integrated into a critical theory oriented to exploring the preconditions and limits of human emancipation.

At another level, or so it seems to me, the pressure from Freudian theory becomes more compelling. Habermas criticizes mechanistic assumptions in Freudian theory which allowed Freud to anticipate a possible future in which patients could be restored to mental health simply by taking a pill. But this anticipated achievement does not necessarily submerge the idea of the subject, for it is conceivable that certain chemical injections (or whatever) could restore an impaired ability to think rationally, to guide conduct by the results of deliberation, and to act responsibly. The treatments might restore mental capacities which had somehow been inhibited; but not, if they were properly selective, themselves control the results of the agent's deliberations and decisions. Freud's anticipation of a future scientific therapy does not undermine the idea of a subject unless it aspires to build into the new therapeutic

3. *Sigmund Freud* (New York: Viking Press, 1971), p. 194.

process controls over the processes of deliberation. And there is no reason to believe that Freud held the latter view.[4]

A Freudian might also criticize Habermas for ignoring the distinction between primary and secondary repression. Primary repression occurs during infancy and takes the form of a fixation. Since the repressing infant lacks clear concepts and beliefs, these repressed contents are not in principle available to adult consciousness, or at least they cannot be closely articulated. If Freudian theory is correct in this respect, then it establishes limits in principle to the ideal of a fully transparent subject. Habermas would have to concede—to look ahead to issues about to be discussed—that even under ideal conditions of discourse, certain components of our emotional lives would remain outside the reach of ratiocination. Such a concession, when its implications are pursued, suggests defects in the rational ideal of discourse Habermas adopts. For it may be necessary to adopt rhetorical devices which encourage subjects of discourse to experience the limits of rational discourse itself. And this implication is antithetical to the Habermasian insistence that discourse be open to everything but the limits of reason.

Psychoanalytic reservations about the Habermasian project revolve around the suspicion that his rationalism insufficiently acknowledges deep and intractable limits to the ideal of the self-transparent subject. Habermas can offer at least two responses. First, these limits themselves are to be recognized through some process of rational deliberation. Habermas may have this point in mind when he says, "no one can know (today) the degree to which aggressiveness can be curtailed" (330), with its corollary that any closer demarcation of those limits will itself be an achievement of rational subjects who have come to understand their "inner nature" more fully. Second, Habermas can remind psychoanalytic theorists that they may distort both their own findings and their comprehension of his orientation by looking primarily in one direction for limits to subjectivity. A theory of intersubjectivity, underdeveloped in Freudian theory, also treats the free subject as a partial

4. Wollheim could be referring to Habermas (though he in fact is not) when he says: "It is often said of the 'Project' that its effect was wholly baneful," blinding "Freud to the significance of intentions, aims, motives, desires in human nature," and strengthening in him "a conception of the mind as a machine subject to casual laws of the utmost simplicity." But, Wollheim contends, "the 'Project' did not equate the mind with a machine. What it did was to use a mechanical model to represent and explain the workings of the mind. And if it went beyond this, it only did so to insist that there is a physiological substrate to psychological phenomena and this substrate must ultimately be understood." Ibid., pp. 55-56.

The Critical Theory of Jürgen Habermas

and vulnerable human achievement. We swim in a sea of socially established preconceptions and assumptions; and at any particular time much of this background must remain outside the range of self-conscious scrutiny. The ideal of the free subject thus presupposes a background of shared orientations which limit realization of the ideal. A more explicit realization that subjectivity is limited in two directions, vertically by unconscious processes and horizontally by an intersubjective background, might allow psychoanalysts to loosen further the structural theory of the unconscious.

It may seem strained to pay attention to relations between the Habermasian project and psychoanalytic theory, since Habermas has given the topic so little attention in his latest work. But that is the rationale for doing so. For, as Habermas has explored a series of issues in theories of socialization and cognitive development, he has provided needed correctives to psychoanalytic theory (for example, it needs a richer theory of cognitive development) while losing some of the dynamic characteristics required by his own theory of psychosocial development. Thus the theory of personal identity Habermas wishes to construct, in which "personality systems find their unity in identity securing interpretive systems" (372), must specify not only those capacities which persons qua persons have as agents capable of assimilating and assessing critically interpretative systems; it must also explain how persons maturing in the same social milieu are individuated, how each acquires an identity which is uniquely his or hers. A dynamic theory of the unconscious contributes to this requirement; it can help Habermas to avoid the "oversocialized" conception of persons which often emerges from social theories of personal identity. Habermas, of course, does transcend one fundamental defect in such oversocialized conceptions. For his role bearers possess the reflective capacity to assess critically the beliefs and norms which help to constitute established roles. But a theory can be oversocialized in another respect. It can fail to discern how an individual's distinctive orientation in one sphere of life, say, one's tendency to trust or distrust associates, is manifested as well in one's orientation to sexuality, interpretation of politics, and sense of humor. Freud may exaggerate slightly when he says that "a man's attitude in sexual life has the force of a model to which the rest of his reactions conform,"[5] but the aphorism does identify one of the ways in which a coherent and distinctive personality is formed.

5. Ibid., p. 135.

Hermeneutics and Emancipation

Habermas recognizes that theorists such as Hans Gadamer and Peter Winch, who pay close attention to the concepts, beliefs, and aspirations of those who enter into social relations, are able to penetrate deeply into the structure of social relations. To understand a way of life, they contend, is to be able to individuate actions as the participants do, and to individuate actions one must place them in the larger social context in which they are situated. Thus to identify the act of plagiarism, one must first know how intellectual life is constituted in contemporary society, what its point or purpose is, and why contributions to that activity are prized by participants. And once "plagiarism" has been placed in this context, one has already gone some distance toward explaining why the activity is condemned by participants.

It is because Habermas recognizes the intersubjective dimension of social life that he is able to plumb the depths of the legitimacy crisis facing advanced capitalist societies today. If institutional practices are partially constituted by shared concepts and beliefs, the loss of identification with those orientations on the part of participants will weaken their performance. It is not just that the motives to carry out established role expectations are now weakened, though that is important enough. But if a traditional set of comon purposes no longer appears clear to the participants or worthy of their allegiance, the explicit rules governing specific role performances also become less and less determinate in their meaning. To have doubts, for instance, about the point of intellectual life as it is presently constituted in our society would be to increase one's doubts about what is to count as an act of plagiarism and how one should react to actions falling within this category. If such doubts arise concerning the role of the welfare state in the civilization of productivity, the implicit understandings and purposes which have traditionally sustained the explicit rules of citizenship and representation will begin to dissipate. And controversies will proliferate over the precise meaning of explicit rules governing tax payments, welfare expenditures, equal opportunity, the rights and duties of parents, the discretionary use of public funds, occupational rewards for merit, and conflicts of interest. The depletion of the intersubjective background to explicit norms brings with it an increase in litigious activity and a decrease in the supply of civic virtue available to the state in playing its role.

Hermeneutic or interpretative theory, then, makes an indispensable contribution to Habermas' version of critical theory. In transcending the thin theory of legitimacy available to empiricists, it allows the critical theorist to probe the inner connections among erosion of institutional legitimacy, the indeterminacy of institutional norms, the depletion of needed motives, and the deterioration of institutional performance. But Habermas must also object to a variety of tendencies in interpretative theory.

First, a pure theory of interpretation carries the implication that the constraints of reason and evidence are in principle insufficient to reduce the number of defensible interpretations of a particular society to one. For if the concepts and beliefs which enter into a way of life are loosely textured and if they are continually open to internal contestation and revision, there is no precisely demarcated evidential base against which to test rival interpretative accounts. More than one interpretation is defensible within the same domain. Gadamer insists on this implication; and it seems to follow as well from points Winch makes in one of his definitive essays.[6]

But Habermas hopes that a single theoretical account might be established as the correct account of a particular society. The pluralism of legitimate interpretations, he believes, generates pernicious consequences for the logic of practical judgment. To eliminate in principle the prospect of one true account available to all rational agents is to sanction ethical pluralism. The doctrine of ethical pluralism in turn weakens the self-confidence of social critics and increases the already impressive leverage available to those who obscure and defend established practices of oppression.

Second, interpretative theorists such as Winch and Gadamer do not appreciate sufficiently the potential importance of the dialectic of self-consciousness in social life. Once established practices—practices endowed by participants with a naturelike status—are seen to be conventional and alterable arrangements, once the established norms of legitimacy and justice are seen to rest on assumptions which have not been fully redeemed by reason, more reflective orientations to these practices can emerge. "In gasping the genesis of the tradition from which it proceeds and on which it turns back, reflection shakes the dogmatism of life practice" (181). Critical self-consciousness opens tradition to reasoned acceptance or to criticism and pressure for reconstitution in the light of reason. In either case the achievement is uniquely human and worthy of our pursuit.

Gadamer, seen from the perspective of Habermas, would leave too much of social life in the shadows. His readiness to do so reflects his failure to comprehend sufficiently how linguistically mediated tradi-

---

6. See Peter Winch, "Understanding a Primitive Society," in Bryan Wilson, ed., *Rationality* (Oxford: Blackwell, 1970).

tions can cut in two directions: the norms which bind a populace into a coherent whole can also sustain the bondage of one segment of a populace within the social whole.

It is a commonplace among political theorists today to say that a society can have civic virtue when its citizens identify unreflectively with a common way of life, and it can have civil liberty when its citizens self-consciously distance themselves from the state; but no society can hope to combine self-consciousness with civic virtue, or civil liberty with *civitas*. The Habermasian treatment of self-consciousness and civic virtue as components within a single ideal of social life appropriate to the contemporary age poses, in my judgment, a profound challenge to this orthodoxy. For, given the extension of literacy, the ready accessibility of public media of communication, the close interdependence among nation-states, and the expanded use of social theory by social planners, the knowledge that one's own way of life is one among a small set of historical possibilities is potentially available to the contemporary citizen. This potentiality for a comparatively high degree of self-consciousness could be curtailed only by repressive means. And, given the necessarily enlarged sphere for social coordination in modern life, a comparatively high level of civic virtue is required to avoid the extension of coordination through coercive control. The ideal of *enlightened civic virtue* which Habermas seeks to sustain may not be fully or neatly realizable; indeed, I shall later suggest that his ideal of self-consciousness needs to be modified significantly. But the aspiration which informs it reflects an understanding of the contemporary condition surpassing both that of those contemporaries who celebrate the primacy of tradition and that of those who celebrate the primacy of individual rights. Each of these alternative viewpoints serves as a mirror to obstruct the vision of the other, and each inadvertently supports the escalation of coercive controls in contemporary politics. The concern to construct a theory of enlightened civic virtue, and to formulate an ideal of political discourse which could today sustain it, stands at the center of the Habermasian problematic. His attraction and antipathy to hermeneutics turn upon its ambiguous relationship to this agenda.

There is a third defect in interpretative theory. It tends to deflate the structural dimension of social life, to obscure how specific practices of production, exchange, stratification, work incentives, labor mobility, and political accountability mutually constrain and enable one another, so that no single practice can be reconstituted significantly unless corollary changes are introduced in the others to which it is linked. The identification of structural constraints in a social order implies that the freedom of its participants is limited in particular directions. If they fail to perceive these limits, their shared self-interpretations mystify the conditions of their own existence even while they help to constitute them.

These three defects in interpretative theory are mutually reinforcing. Failure to recognize the structural constraints inherent in a social whole weakens the ability to see how linguistically mediated traditions might serve as a medium of oppression; and the tendency to endorse the self-interpretation of participants, legitimized by the presumption that freedom consists in the internalization of established tradition, weakens the theoretical incentive to seek universally valid standards of social critique. The comparative absence in interpretative theory of political categories such as ideology, power, struggle, and oppression is a symptom of these deficiencies in its social epistemology. Seen from the perspective of Habermas, to correct these three defects is to generate the imperative to criticize ideologies which mystify portions of our social existence. And the critique of ideology generates the aspiration to ground critical theory in reason. The issues are thus sharply joined. But to resolve them entirely in favor of critical theory, Habermas must reach the ground which slipped away in *Knowledge and Human Interests*.

The Theory of Communication

Whoever criticizes or endorses the assumptions and norms in a way of life affirms the validity of certain criteria of theoretical and practical judgment. The theory of communication is an attempt to elucidate a mode of discourse which will first incorporate the correct criteria and then generate the correct result.

The frame for this inquiry is stated in Habermas' inaugural lecture at Frankfurt University in 1965: "the human interest in autonomy and responsibility is not mere fancy, for it can be apprehended *a priori*. . . . Our first sentence expresses unequivocally the intention of universal and unconstrained consensus" (287). Habermas signals there his intention to formulate a modified version of the transcendental argument.

McCarthy surveys the emerging theory of universal pragmatics whereby Habermas delineates universal capacities and standards implied by a variety of speech acts. I shall focus on two aspects of that project: the consensus theory of truth and the model of practical discourse.

If correspondence theories of truth are damaged by our realization that there is no theory-neutral data base *sufficient* to adjudicate between rival theories, and if coherence theories are similarly jeoparadized by the implication that more than one theory in a "given" domain can meet the relevant tests of coherence, perhaps a consensus theory can fill the void. It treats as true statements which would gain the assent of all others under specified conditions of communication. But such a theory, McCarthy reminds us, is open to a standard objection. Thus, if we can state the conditions (or criteria) for ascertaining the truth of an achieved consensus, then these criteria, and not the consensus, assume central importance; and if we cannot specify such criteria, we have shown no way (or perhaps no formalizable way) to distinguish a grounded from an ungrounded consensus. Habermas recognizes this dilemma. He seeks to escape it by articulating certain conditions of discourse, the ideal speech situation; these conditions set a frame within which reasoned discourse can produce truth, even though they do not themselves uniquely determine the truth. The truth is those conclusions about "inner" and "outer" nature which emerge unscathed from such a discourse *and* which would continue to emerge in any future discourse meeting the specified conditions.

There is something attractive about this effort. It speaks to our intuition that, in social inquiry at least, the processes of discovery and creation are not neatly separable. We know both that the concepts and beliefs we have about ourselves help to constitute our relations and that these orientations must recognize a set of constraints posed by inner and outer nature if they are to escape distortion. Habermas seeks to bring both of these intuitions within the frame of one theory of truth. He acknowledges the first by reference to an intersubjective consensus and the second by reference to certain parameters of discourse which constrain but do not uniquely determine it. That is, at least, how I now understand his theory.

It does seem to me, nonetheless, that the dilemma he seeks to escape may have been shifted onto a new terrain. If the conditions of ideal speech (the symmetrical distribution of chances to enter into dialogue, the effective opportunity for all participants to call into question unexamined presuppositions in a discourse, the suspension of all motives except the desire to reach a rational conclusion) are loosely defined, then there is no assurance that *one* truth will emerge in each domain of inquiry. If the conditions are specified closely, it becomes contestable— and thus legitimately part of the discourse itself—whether these conditions are in fact met in a specific discourse or whether they themselves are unduly restrictive. What presents itself as an ideal speech situation from one vantage point (say Marxian theory) may appear as a subtly distorted discourse from another (say Freudian theory). And the discourse over these questions will be pursued within contested parameters of discourse.

The mode of ideal discourse which now emerges is as close to the hermeneutic circle as it is to the ideal speech situation. This alternative ideal of discourse presupposes a standard of truth, but in any particular time and place its pursuit requires preliminary acceptance of a particular set of prejudices within which the discourse proceeds. *Any* of the latter may be called into question at a particular time, but *some* set must be accepted while the others are called into question. Unless some set is assumed, we lack sufficient resources to generate determinate conclusions; but if some particular subset of potentially contestable claims must provide the unexamined background of any particular discourse, we are never guaranteed that its conclusions are untainted by prejudice. It is a faulty abstraction to extrapolate from a series of such discourses to a cumulative result which is both true and rich enough to generate specific results.

I am not at all sure that Habermas would thoroughly disagree with these last comments. He seems to hold that practical limits of space, time, psychology (and convention?) ensure that the pure conditions of discourse will never be attained, but that the ideal is nonetheless worthy of our acceptance. As McCarthy puts it, "our history is replete with ideals—religious, ethical, political, cognitive, artistic—that we know to be incapable of complete realization but that are no less effective in shaping social life" (310). And Habermas believes that we must presuppose such an ideal every time we enter into actual discourse—since we construe ourselves to be subjects able to be moved by the force of the better argument.

The question becomes, then: do compelling arguments against the possibility in principle of realizing the pure conditions of discourse undermine the standard, or merely expose limits in our ability to reach the truth and know that we have done so? Similarly, has Habermas, in equating truth with an ideal consensus, committed a category mistake, treating an exploration into the conditions of rational judgment as if it were one into the meaning of truth? I am not ready to pose an answer to these questions. An informed reply will take seriously the Nietzschean charge that none of the established theories of truth work because truth is form imposed by humans upon material not designed to receive it. The Habermasian theory is clearly designed to provide an answer to the Nietzschean perspective, but it is now more of a promise than an answer.

But perhaps a less ambitious question can be answered now; for if the conditions of actual discourse must always fall short of the model idealized by Habermas, and if social life is constituted in part by self-interpretations which grow out of actual discourse, then the persistent failure to reach consensus in social theory is not *necessarily* a sign of irrationality (or a low level of rationality) on the part of some participants or of repressive constraints which unjustifiably confine the possibilities for discursive validation of claims. It may be. But typically, such contentions themselves will be inherently contestable, embodying projections about future possibilities which are not now susceptible to definitive resolution by participants. And this impasse might persist even if all parties were to suspend (or try to suspend) ulterior motives while examining claims and counterclaims. The realization that the conclusions of actual discourse are always problematic to some degree carries political implications for critical theory. For the political action sanctioned by critical reflection must be tempered by the understanding that the critique itself rests upon foundations that are themselves contestable.

The Legitimation Crisis

McCarthy closes the discussion of Habermas' theory of practical discourse with a quotation which summarizes its aspiration and points toward the Habermasian theory of tendencies toward legitimacy crisis in advanced capitalist society. In appraising the practices of a society, Habermas says, we must pose the counterfactual question "How would the members of a social system, at a given stage in the development of productive forces, have collectively and bindingly interpreted their needs (and which norms would they have accepted as justified) if they could and would have decided on the organization of social intercourse through discursive will-formation, with adequate knowledge of the limiting conditions and functional imperatives of their society?" (332) The very audacity of the question tends to put one off. But this reaction must be tempered by the reminder, first, that even audacious questions can be answered cautiously and tentatively and, second, that this question, or its functional equivalent, is posed implicitly every time we support or challenge the legitimacy of established institutions. Habermas asks it of the way of life sustained within advanced capitalist systems and emerges with a theory of legitimation crisis tendencies.

Advanced capitalist societies, Habermas believes, may be able to cope with the economic dislocations they generate, but to do so the state must progressively "steer" the economy more closely and overtly. The enlarged state, in turn, may be able to steer the economy in a technical sense, but it faces more difficulties in regenerating the *motives* people require to work efficiently and to carry out effectively a variety of private and public roles essential to the performance of the system. The processes of capital accumulation have eroded the traditional social bases of these motives, and the state is limited in its ability to restore these bases or to produce new motives. As the state necessarily and progressively intercedes into areas traditionally outside its sphere, its difficulties in sustaining its own legitimacy increase. The difficulties are of two, related, types. First, the state may not be able to act effectively to meet the established expectations of many constituencies to which it is formally accountable, for it is limited by constraints imposed by the very terms of relation between it and the privately incorporated economy. Second, and more fundamentally, the established norms themselves, if they were to come up for public reconsideration in a discourse free from domination, would not be justified as in the best interests of those now guided by them. The continued legitimacy of established norms depends on their continued mystification, but the very visibility of the state makes that mystification more difficult. Technocratic images of politics and administration do depoliticize and legitimize to some degree, but they may not be as effective in the long run as the image of the market was in an earlier phase of capitalism.

The detailed presentation of these themes is fascinating and, in my view, always relevant to an assessment of the dialetical relation between the growth of state activity and its declining legitimacy in the eyes of those to whom it is accountable. I will merely pose a couple of questions here.

If advanced capitalism could not sustain its legitimacy under conditions of free and informed discourse, why is the welfare state in fact singled out to be the principal target of explicit disaffection? Put more closely, if an entire set of practices and objectives (such as instrumental work, the treatment of the elderly, the dissolution of city life, environmental degradation, extensive stratification) would not be justified if participants were fully aware of how each element in this complex requires the others and how the entire complex promises to undermine the prospects of a good life for future generations, why is the covert disaffection from these practices projected overtly onto the welfare state? Habermas' excursion into theories of socialization and congnitive development suggests that he would not be happy with explanations which stress indoctrination and manipulation by ruling elites. Such theories do not mesh well with empirical evidence about the selective reception of media messages. Moreover, such a theory does not square with the contrasting model of communicative dialogue posed by Habermas. How could the populace be so passive and irrational now and so active and rational in a hypothetical future?

I believe that a theory of personal identity can help account for this phenomenon in a way consistent with the larger outline of Habermas' theory. If a blue-collar worker, rearing a family, wishes to see himself as dignified and free; if he wishes to interpret his life activity as supportive of his children's chances to escape the conditions in which he finds himself, then he must give some legitimacy to the established ideal of equal opportunity. It is the gate through which his children might pass into the good life. And if the ideal of equal opportunity is to be viable in this society, it is important to subscribe to at least some of the ends which can be attained by passing through that gate. In this way (and many others), the desire to identify oneself as acting effectively to promote the future prospect of one's children encourages one to identify overtly with a set of institutions and goals, even if one's concrete behavior reflects covert disenchantment with those same institutions and goals. In such a context, the state, as the one institution of public accountability, as one institution which must support the performance of the economy when it falters, emerges as the screen upon which a deeper, unacknowledged disaffection can be projected. Because it is the agency of public accountability, we can construe ourselves to be free as a people only if we can believe that state officials could, if they were more honest or competent, steer the economy more effectively. Indeed, to see ourselves as potentially free, free as a people, we are encouraged to redefine issues and grievances so that they fall within the ambit of legitimate state authority. We then blame the state for unnecessary ineptness within the prevailing order, for that orientation holds out the possibility that new state officials might do the job more effectively and competently. Our covert disaffection from the civilization of productivity is expressed in such behavioral trends as deteriorating worker motivation, high divorce rates, increased drug use, the growth of the litigious personality, the withdrawal into fundamentalist religion, child abuse, and the escalation of violent crime, while our explicit expressions of disaffection are concentrated on the one institution which is formally accountable to the electorate.

If this thesis were pursued relentlessly, one could argue that the latent disaffection from the civilization of productivity is expressed as the disenchantment from the welfare state because such a resolution is most consistent with the quest for personal identity available to a large range of participants. Such a thesis would not suffice to account for the discrepancy between the covert signs of disaffection and the actual articulation of public issues. But it would help.

The Critical Theory of Jürgen Habermas

One further consideration is also pertinent. Effective political expression of this disaffection from the priorities and role requirements of the civilization of productivity would presuppose the viability of some version of socialism. For in the absence of a viable alternative it is rational to reconcile oneself to the limits of this system. But historical experience does not provide reassuring support for such an alternative. And socialist theorists, even at the level of speculative theory, have not offered a vision of socialism which speaks convincingly to the issues of freedom and democratic control while maintaining contact with the complexities of contemporary social life. Given this uneven development in socialist theory, there is a certain rationality in the failure of disaffected constituencies to convert their covert disenchantment into a political program. The logic of legitimation itself supports resignation to established practices until a convincing image of democratic socialism can be discerned. Those who think, as I do, that today such resignation carries repressive political implications have a special obligation to explore new versions of socialist theory.

Habermas' theory of legitimation crisis tendencies in advanced capitalist states exudes an air of pessimism. As McCarthy points out, the analysis does not locate a particular constituency "whose interest it might seek to articulate" (385) and who might become the agent of progressive historical change. This is a version of critical theory without a specific constituency, and yet it is also a version which provokes and grips many readers. We are provoked by the effort to clarify the preconditions of enlightened politics, and we are gripped by the fear that these preconditions themselves may be susceptible to further dissolution. One possible response to the disparity between the imperatives of capitalist accumulation and the declining ability of these imperatives to secure the reflective allegiance of the populace is a further withdrawal into privatism. An unreflective citizenry could concentrate its attention elsewhere while it passively accepted new regulations and ignored new sacrifices and disciplines imposed upon minorities inessential to the productive system. Habermas does not announce this possibility, but his criticisms of a variety of theoretical traditions do revolve around tendencies within each to repudiate or downgrade the importance of self-consciousness and enlightenment in contemporary politics. These theories, it is feared, could help to legitimize a movement to disconnect state activity from effective accountability. Systems theorists— Lühmann is the leading example—provide the most blatant instance, for they would increase state effectiveness by freeing it from the obligation to defend the rationale for its policies to a wider audience. But other traditions, contributing elements essential to critical theory, are not exempt from such criticisms. Freudian theorists define the limits to freedom required by civilization as such but ignore the threat to civilization posed by the priorities of our political economy; hermeneuticists express nostalgia for traditional modes of thought and practice while sliding over the structural imperatives of the contemporary order; Marxists of positivist and structuralist inclinations construct theories in which the idea of the subject is treated as a myth and people are treated as the mere bearers of socially produced roles. If the portraits of these theories are exaggerated, the exaggerations are illuminating. They point to analogues at the level of theory to pressures in contemporary politics to close the space for a politics of enlightenment.

The ideal of discursive rationality, serving as the centerpiece of Habermas' theory, is more than an abstract theoretical construct. It symbolizes at once the ideal of enlightened politics and the threatened closure of public space for its realization. Unconstrained by any concrete political practice, it provides a sanctuary of sorts for political reflection. In this space thought could run idle, even if politics ran out of control. We have here the idealized speech of stoics frozen out of effective participation in public life. The wish to expand the space for democratic politics and the anxiety that democratic political discourse may become increasingly detached from the concrete imperatives of our political economy are condensed into the symbol of ideal speech.

6

THE DILEMMA OF

LEGITIMACY

In our times we can neither endure our faults nor the means of correcting them.

—Livy

In a highly structured order, people tend to be pulled simultaneously by one wish to identify with established norms and another to evade or resist onerous claims made upon them. Some are drawn exclusively toward one of these poles, but many others are torn between them. The latter will endorse law and order belligerently and cheat on their income taxes, or express anarchistic impulses and raise their children to be lawyers, or insist that the government get off the backs of the people and support policies which extend surveillance over marginal constituencies. The tensions here are not merely psychological; they embody attempts to meet the claims of the self and the claims of order in a setting which makes it difficult to do both.

The classical doctrine of liberalism projected a vision of social life which honored both sets of claims. Endorsing a general set of constitutional rules which all citizens were to obey, it entrusted a broad range of conduct to the impersonal control of the market and placed the remainder within a private sphere beyond the normal reach of direct public control. The liberal ideal never harmonized closely with the actual organization of private and public life, but the fit was close enough to allow its supporters to help define the form and limits of operative public authority.

The attraction of the liberal doctrine resided largely in its desire to acknowledge together the claims of public authority and private prerogative. But, as its conceptual resources have lagged behind changes in the structure of modern life, this attraction has faded. The web of social life is now too tightly drawn to sustain this picture of public authority and private refuge. The current proclivity to characterize behavior once thought to be eccentric as mental illness in need of medical care presents merely one sign of the penetration of public-private bureaucracies into the inner citadels of private life. Put another way, a broad range of private activities and social practices must today be coordinated (to use a neutral term) by public means; and a large number of people unable or unwilling to comply voluntarily with official expectations are now subjected to legal controls, therapeutic counsel, and incentive systems to bring their conduct in line with the limits of the order.

As the web of social discipline has tightened, other familiar doctrines of the nineteenth and twentieth centuries have also begun to seem vaguely disconnected from our current condition. Critics who appeal to a communitarian ideal of life or gesture toward anarchism illuminate features of our life otherwise left in the shadows, but the counterideals they pose lack specificity and credibility. Pressed very hard by communitarians or anarchists, most of us retreat toward liberal standards of citizenship, freedom, and privacy. And yet when the liberal, inflated by success in piercing these pretensions, attempts to woo us back to the liberal camp, we discern even more poignantly how the doctrine draws a veil of ignorance across the most disturbing features of contemporary life.

This condition can be generalized across the entire landscape of contemporary theoretical discourse. Dissident perspectives demystify features of the established order, but then condense into a light mist of lofty ideals; and the operative ideals, which retain some ability to set limits to the morally tolerable in the existing order, rest on assumptions and perceptions increasingly at odds with established realities. Political theorists thus find themselves wandering through the debris of old doctrines, searching for stray material from which to construct new understandings. These features of current political theory, I contend, are themselves symptoms of the dilemma of legitimacy which is beginning to emerge in our civilization.

How should we try to pick our way through this field? My own effort is informed by the following judgment: the categories supplied by a collectivist theory of legitimacy provide the most refined instruments with which to probe subterranean developments in our civilization, but these instruments themselves must be redesigned once that excavation is finished, once we begin digging our way out. In defending this perspective, I first delineate a collectivist conception of legitimacy which transcends the thin conception governing much current social theory, next define the contours of a dilemma of legitimacy which is beginning to take shape in American politics, then examine briefly two theories which are themselves symptoms of this development, and last confront an alternate perspective which might allow us to correct the repressive tendencies implicit within the collectivist problematic of legitimacy.

The Dilemma of Legitimacy

The Question of Legitimacy

A thin theory of legitimacy continues to inform most accounts of current politics. It assumes that allegiance to the order is intact unless there is overt, widespread, and well-articulated opposition to it; that belief in the legitimacy of the order is equivalent to the order's legitimacy; that the beliefs most pivotal to the question of legitimacy are those concerning the constitutive principles of the political process; and that since the ends governing our civilization are inherently rational they could not themselves become illegitimate. Few theorists accept all of these provisions today. But a variety of recent theorists, representing diverse ideological positions, adopt one or more of them when posing questions about the legitimacy of the order.[1]

The thin conception of legitimacy misconstrues the way in which social relations and institutions are constituted. Misreading the constitutive dimensions of social life, it may be able to detect certain symptoms of a withdrawal of allegiance from the order, but it lacks the conceptual resources to comprehend the internal structure of that order or to assess its potential import.

A healthy order, from the vantage point of its participants, is a way of life which promotes the good we share in common; the limits it imposes are tolerable to most because they are thought to be necessary to the common good it fosters. To participate in such a way of life is to carry an enormous load of prejudgments embodied in the common language and solidified in institutional practices. One's personal identity is intimately bound up with the larger way of life: that identity provides one with the density needed to maintain social relations, to form practical judgments, and to criticize specific feature of the common life.

This is an incomplete picture of any way of life. (For instance, its structural dimension has been ingnored.) But it is complete enough to allow us to relocate the question of legitimacy. First, if the preunderstandings implicit in social relations seriously misconstrue the range of possibilities inherent in the order, expressions of allegiance at one moment will rest upon a series of illusions which may become apparent at a future moment. The historical course of development actually open

---

1. See: Daniel Bell, *The Cultural Contradictions of Capitalism* (New York: Basic Books, 1976); James O'Connor, *The Fiscal Crisis of the State* (New York: St. Martin's Press, 1973); Theodore Lowi, *The End of Liberalism* (New York: W.W. Norton, 1968); George Kateb, "On the 'Legitimation Crisis,'" *Social Research* 46, no. 4 (Winter 1979): 695-727; and Erik Olin Wright, *Class, Crisis and the State* (London: New Left Books, 1978).

to the order may ensure that future generations will become disenchanted with it.

Second, a widespread commitment to the constitutional principles of the political order may be matched by distantiation from the role imperatives governing everyday life. In a highly structured order, the withdrawal of allegiance in this second sphere will carry profound implications for the performance of the economy, the tax levels required by the state, the scope of the state's police functions, and the ability of the state to bear the burdens imposed upon it. It may, in short, impair the state's ability to play its legitimate role in the current order of things.

Third, the ends and purposes fostered by an order can themselves become objects of disaffection. Hegel explored instances when a set of priorities which once gripped a populace lose their credibility as the negative dimensions in them become more fully visible to later generations. Such a contradictory tendency embodies a historical dimension whereby abstract goals inspire a populace at one moment but decline in their ability to secure reflective allegiance once their actual content becomes clear through cumulative experience. If the institutional complex sustaining these purposes has solidified, we might expect expressions of disaffection to be more symptomatic than articulate and more covert than overt. The lack of any sense of credible alternatives operates to limit the political definition of the new sense of disenchantment, but its emergence nonetheless affects the performance of the institutional complex.

But why such an emphasis on the symptomatic, the covert, the indirect, and the unarticulated when pursuing the question of legitimacy? Because, fourth, the identities of the participants are bound up with the institutions in which they are implicated. The modern individual, possessing the capacity for self-consciousness, is never exhausted by any particular set of roles. But one's sense of dignity, of self-identity, is intimately linked to one's ability to endorse the way of life one actually lives.

This relation between personal identity and institutional practice complicates the question of legitimacy. To become severely disaffected from that which one is called upon to do in work, family, and consumption is also to become disaffected from the self one has become. When the distance between what one is and what one does is great, one is likely to hold oneself in contempt. For one must now either appear to be unfree (acting only under duress) or appear deceitful (pretending to endorse roles experienced as hateful). In either case, one feels cast off from oneself, anxious and demoralized.

The situation is not helped if the experience is joined to the conviction that little can be done to remedy it through politics. One way to save appearances in such a setting is to reconnect rhetorically that which is disconnected in practice. Some politicians understand how difficult circumstances can foster collective self-deception or, better described, the careful cultivation of a shared innocence about the historical course a people is on. "They want to believe, that is the point isn't it?" So Nixon whispered to Haldeman and the tape recorder when they were assessing his chances of overcoming the mass of evidence piling up against him. He understood the close relation between the quest for personal identity and the will to believe that all is right with the world.

Because these connections can be so intimate, a theory of legitimacy must probe the implicit, the unacknowledged, and the symptomatic as well as that which is acknowledged and articulated. And because it must do so, any particular account is bound to be controversial and problematic in some respects. This result resides more in the character of the object of inquiry than in the defective design of the theoretical perspective governing inquiry into it. The philosophical recognition of this feature of modern life carries political implications. It provides, as it were, philosophical space for politics. It identifies politics as the sphere of the unsettled, as the mode of social relations which properly emerges when issues require resolution and the available resources of reason and evidence are insufficient to settle them.

The question of legitimacy is important to us because we wish to live, to the extent possible in any complex, modern society, as free agents in an order which deserves our allegiance and is responsive to our deepest grievances and criticisms. It is also important because we sense that politics, in the best sense of that term, requires a background of public allegiance to the most basic principles governing the order. The thin conception of legitimacy appears to avoid a series of perplexing issues posed by acceptance of the alternate perspective. That is also its defect. It converts the concern behind the question of legitimacy into a set of more manageable and trivial questions.

Productivity and Legitimacy

Two fundamental sets of priorities have governed the American civilization. It seeks to sustain an economy of growth so that each generation can be more prosperous, secure, and comfortable than its predecessor. And it seeks to support a constitutional democracy in which the state is accountable to its citizens and the citizens have rights against the state. The first priority is expressed in the organization of work, profit, property, and consumption which typifies the society. These practices are constituted in part by the standards of efficiency, cost effectiveness, productivity, punctuality, and consumer satisfaction inherent in them. The second priority is reflected in our concern with human rights, freedom, the entitlements of citizenship, and competitive elections. Its constitution involves the readiness of participants to see themselves as citizens and to carry out the prerogatives of citizenship.

The legitimacy of the entire order involves, first, the ability of each set of priorities to retain the reflective allegiance of most citizens and, second, the continued ability of each priority to exist in harmony with the other.

I believe that the first set of institutions and priorities, the civilization of productivity, is progressively losing its credibility as its imperatives become more deeply entrenched. The decline in credibility involves a process of disillusionment in which the institutional pursuit of a set of ends once thought to be self-evident begins to appear more and more as self-defeating to new generations. In turn, the disillusionment adversely affects the ability of the institutions to promote these ends by noncoercive means. Since the institutional forms which constitute the order are now solidified, since they now form an interdependent structure in which none can be reconstituted very thoroughly without corollary shifts in the constitution of the others, this disaffection is not likely to find clear political expression. Its political articulation tends to be displaced. The disaffection does, though, take its toll in the civilization of productivity. It also increases the burdens imposed upon the welfare state, the one institution which is accountable to the electorate. The long-term effect strains the ability of the state to retain democratic accountability. The erosion of legitimacy in the one sphere eventually contaminates the legitimacy of the other.

What, more concretely, is involved in this experience of disillusionment? First, it becomes more apparent to consumers that the pursuit of universal private affluence, full of promise during its early stages, eventually generates a self-defeating dialectic. The economy may produce riches, but the good life contained within the ideal of "affluence" seems to recede constantly into the horizon. Goods introduced initially as luxuries or conveniences later become necessary objects of consumption, and much of their initial charm is lost.

As described earlier, this conversion process is propelled partly by the changes in the social infrastructure of consumption which must accompany each significant change in the social composition of consumption goods.[2] These changes in the infrastructure of consumption not only convert the initial luxury into an expensive necessity of consumption, but they tend to reduce pleasure in the use of the vehicle. Many of the paradigmatic goods of the affluent society, because they are built around the assumption of private consumption, decline in value as they are extended to more people. Private resorts, technical education, suburban living, and the automobile decline in value as they are universalized, partly because much of their initial value resided in the exclusivity of their possession and partly because the setting in which they are consumed normally deteriorates as they are universalized. If these goods (representing the paradigm goods of the affluent society) were to be restricted, the end of universal affluence which helps to legitimate the civilization of productivity would be jeopardized. But if they were indeed extended to everyone, the achievement of "affluence" itself would contradict the hopes which inspired earlier generations to pursue it.

If the universalization of affluence is one of the ends which legitimize the role imperatives governing the civilization of productivity, and if that end is now seen by many to contain illusory expectations, everyday allegiance to role assignments will deteriorate. The reaction, experienced as growing skepticism about the system's ability to universalize the good life it pursues, does not expunge the desire for consumption goods, for to opt out of the expansionary process is to worsen one's own comparative position. But it does weaken the willingness to impose disciplines upon oneself at work, home, and school.

Suspicions arise in other areas as well. Institutions, standards, and norms which once seemed conducive to private welfare and public good now present a more ambiguous appearance. It begins to appear that the system of labor mobility, which promises to improve the standard of living for many each generation, also operates over the long term to damage cherished ties of kinship and neighborhood; that the stratification system needed to motivate people to fill the lowliest positions also operates persistently to close some segments of the society out of its paradigmatic rewards; that the massive exploitation of natural resources needed to fuel the economy of growth deepens the nation's dependence on resources located in foreign lands; that the established

2. This argument is most cogently developed in: Fred Hirsch, *The Social Limits to Growth* (Cambridge, Mass.: Harvard University Press, 1977). An earlier version, more attuned to the implications for politics and less precise with respect to the self-defeating character of the universalization of affluence, can be found in: Michael Best and William Connolly, *The Politicized Economy,* 2d ed. (Lexington: D. C. Heath, 1981).

forms of investment, production, and work which generate abundance also render the natural environment less hospitable to future human habitation; that the pace of occupational change required to propel perpetual economic growth also renders each generation of workers obsolete just when it reaches the point in the life cycle where its members are most in need of the respect and dignity bestowed on those functionally important to the society; and that the intensification of managerial controls over the work process to increase productivity drains these role assignments of dignity and social significance. The suspicion forms that these are not dispensable "side effects" to a common pursuit which can be carried out without them; rather they are intrinsic to the historical development of the civilization of productivity. They are part of its success, and any sustained effort to eliminate them would undermine the principal aims which the civilization of productivity can promote.

Other civilizations, of course, have faced difficulties in promoting the material welfare of their populations. But that is not the point here. For not many of them were constructed around the promise to universalize private affluence. I am not contending, either, that most people today have a "lower standard of living" than people had two or three generations ago. The contention is rather that the orientation to the future is undergoing significant change. Nostalgia refers less to a past which is thought to have been richer and more secure and more to one which could believe in the future it was building. The nostalgia of today embodies a loss of innocence about the future we are building. As the feeling grows that the fulfillment of the American dream must always recede into the horizon, as it becomes clear that it might even become a nightmare for future generations, identification with the disciplines and sacrifices required to sustain the civilization of productivity is placed under severe strains. These strains in turn weaken the performance of the defining institutions of the civilization.

The relation between the state and the system of productivity works to deflect political articulation of this disillusionment, to increase the burdens imposed upon the state, to deplete the civic resources the state can draw upon in bearing these burdens, and to set up the welfare apparatus of the state as the screen upon which the disaffection is reflected. The welfare state looks in two directions at the same time. It is the agency of public accountability through competitive elections, and it is dependent upon the successful performance of the privately incorporated system of productivity. This dual accountability of the state discourages political articulation of the disillusionment with the civilization of productivity. For the state must foster private productivity to generate tax revenues, and its successful accountability to the electorate depends upon its ability to generate those revenues.

The state is caught in a bind which its citizens actively help to create. Our cherished view of ourselves as free citizens depends upon the belief that the state, as the one institution of public accountability, has sufficient resources to promote common ends and purposes. Its capacity to act effectively is closely bound up with my understanding of myself as a free agent. I see myself as free if the roles I play are congruent with the principles and purposes I adopt upon reflection. If those roles or the purposes they serve were experienced as onerous and oppressive, and if individuals were unsuccessful in defining new ones, their sense of personal freedom would then depend on the ability of the state to reconstitute these established forms. If it could not act even if we wished it to and we were thoroughly disaffected from the drift of our private and public life, then we would have to see ourselves as unfree, as governed more by fate and necessity than by reason and decision. And our collective unfreedom would eventually become the unfreedom of particular individuals as well.

One way to preserve the desired appearance of collective and personal freedom is to define the troubles which grip us to fit within the range of options effectively available to the state in the current order. Victims of inflation, therefore, unable to alter the consumption priorities, shoddy products, expensive style changes, and price markups in the corporate sector, demand what the state can give them: cuts in school budgets and welfare expenditures. They attack those proximate sources of inflation which are subject to public control. Workers in depressed areas, unable to stop runaway companies, call upon the state to expand unemployment benefits and to stimulate the production of new jobs. Citizens, unable to curb the processes which weaken kinship ties, call upon the state to care for the victims of this process (the elderly, the infirm, the mentally ill, and delinquents), even though state agencies cannot care for these dependent constituencies with the dignity needed.

The bind in which the corporate system and its citizens place the state is this: if state policies undermine economic expansion, it loses its economic basis for action; if it acts within these constraints, it increasingly absorbs the dependent constituencies and unprofitable tasks closed out of the privately incorporated economy. It is then unable to meet the standards of efficiency and profitability operative in the private economy or to hold its budget levels down; and it is held responsible for the failure to live up to these expectations.

The state is seen as accountable to the degree that it is seen to be capable of responding to our grievances in the established order. We see ourselves as free, free as a people, to the extent that we define our grievances to fall within the range of its capacity for action. The welfare state thus emerges from this historical process as a depository for clientele closed out of the system of productivity and programs unable to resolve the troubles which it generated. The bloated welfare state is thus set up to be the visible target of public disaffection more deeply rooted in the priorities and practices of the civilization of productivity.

We publicly call upon the state to promote growth, eliminate superfluous public programs, control inflation, and discipline those who siphon off public resources; and we resist privately the specific sacrifices it would impose upon us. The point in calling upon it in general to take those actions is that they fall within its orbit of legitimate action. The point in resisting the specific application of state policies to one's particular constituency flows from the conviction that the roles we bear in the civilization of productivity already constitute sacrifice enough. Anything more becomes unacceptable and unbearable. The cumulative result is a decline in allegiance to the welfare state and an increasing tolerance of state programs designed to intimidate, control, and suppress its former clients. The decline in the legitimacy of the welfare state is joined to allegiance to an abstract idea of the American state in the civilization of productivity. The logic supporting such a combination is this: we are potentially free as long as the existing state bureaucracy is unnecessarily inept; it can be seen as unnecessarily inept as long as we can identify new courses of state action in the prevailing order which promise to transcend the policies of the discredited welfare state. This combination secures the appearance of collective freedom, but it does so by masking a deeper and rational disaffection from the institutional imperatives and priorities of the civilization of productivity.

The preceding summary leaves out themes which would have to be developed in a more complete presentation, but a more complete account would not prove convincing if this brief outline now appears incredible. The framework, I hope, is sufficiently clear to allow me to formulate the crucial elements in the dilemma (or perhaps dilemmas) of legitimacy.

First, the ends fostered by the civilization of productivity no longer can command reflective allegiance of many who are implicated in those institutions, while the consolidation of these institutions into a structure of interdependencies makes it extremely difficult to recast the ends to be pursued. The institutional complex declines in its ability to secure the allegiance of its role bearers once its actual achievements have been experienced; but the practices of work, profit, international trade, consumption, and stratification have solidified into an interdependent structure resistant to serious reconstitution.

Second, it will become increasingly difficult to maintain the performance of the system of productivity, and the policies required to do so will further erode operational allegiance to its roles and priorities. On the one side, the investment funds, disciplinary controls, and resources needed to promote the required rate of growth in an unfavorable environment will be generated by the imposition of austerity on large segments of the populace (if they are generated) and by a further retreat from environmental policies designed to protect the health of the populace. Maintenance of the system of productivity in adverse circumstances thus requires contraction of the paradigmatic benefits it promises to dispense. These selective reductions in affluence, security, and health will further deplete the allegiance of many who are expected to carry out role assignments within the system. On the other side, resistance to these impositions by those without effective market or political leverage (e.g., welfare recipients, workers in the market sector, low- and middle-level public employees, the mentally ill, delinquents, criminals) will encourage an extension of private and public modes of disciplinary control. The deterioration in the performance of the system of productivity, combined with the pressures to mobilize additional resources to maintain its performance, operates eventually to squeeze the space for democratic politics.

Third, if, as I claim, disenchantment with the civilization of productivity is based upon a growing experiential knowledge of illusions inside those pursuits, it is pertinent to ask: what constellation of ends, limits, imperatives, and priorities could a modern populace endorse today as worthy of its allegiance? If a reconstitution of the defining institutions were possible, what direction should the evolutionary changes take? What could replace or temper the ends of the civilization of productivity? The failure to answer this question, even at the level of theory, contributes to the gap between the covert symptoms of disaffection and the overt insistence on supporting established political priorities. In the absence of credible alternatives, there is a certain rationality in holding onto illusions with which we are already familiar. One of the best ways to accomplish that is to cultivate a studied innocence about the historical course we are on.

The first two ingredients in the dilemma of legitimacy press most heavily on those who pretend that democracy and productivity can continue to cohere without undue strain. The third presses critics who believe that the future of democracy requires a reconstitution of the ends and imperatives governing the system of productivity. In what follows, I try to indicate how recent shifts within a variety of theoretical orientations provide indirect acknowledgment of the dilemma posed here; and I use the opportunity to ascertain how each orientation can, though not always intentionally, deepen our understanding of the character of this dilemma.

The Bifurcation of Liberalism

Current liberalism cannot be defined merely through its commitment to freedom, rights, dissent, and justice. It must be understood, as well, through the institutional arrangements it endorses. Its unity grows out of the congruence between these ideals and their institutional supports. If the first principle of liberalism is liberty, the second is practicality. Liberal practicality involves the wish to support policies which appear attainable within the current order; it is the desire to be part of the action, to be "in the middle" of things, to propose policies today which might be instituted tomorrow.

The priorities of liberty and practicality can be united as long as it is possible to believe that the welfare state in the privately incorporated economy of growth can be the vehicle of liberty and justice. Liberalism, so constituted, avoids the dilemma of legitimacy. But if such a dilemma is beginning to shake the ground underneath its feet, we should expect its proponents to acknowledge these shifts somehow, if only indirectly. I think this is happening. Liberalism is increasingly divided against itself. One constellation of liberals subordinates the commitment to practicality to preserve liberal ideals, and the other submerges the ideals to preserve practicality. Neither side acknowledges the dilemma of legitimacy. But the new division is a symptom of its emergence. The bifurcation of liberalism and the dilemma of legitimacy unfold together.

The first constellation, the beautiful souls of our day, strive to find space in the current order where the ideals of virtuous action, freedom, and justice can be preserved. Sometimes following the lead of Hannah Arendt, they strive to close the instrumentalities of labor, interest, profit, and consumption out of the political sphere. These practices and priorities are not to be treated as the materials of politics, properly understood. But because the virtues the new liberals support are increasingly at odds with the way of the world, and because they evade (treat as subordinate and secondary) the deep intrusion of these worldly concerns into political life, the commitment to liberal principles is increasingly matched by the disengagement from practical issues. The principles themselves tend to become more abstract, more difficult to articulate specifically or to link to particular questions.[3]

The gradual retreat from practicality is principled; the abstract voice of virtue does help to set the limits of the morally tolerable in the existing order. Its voice is not, therefore, to be demeaned or ridiculed. But this principled liberalism is neither at home in the civilization of productivity nor prepared to challenge its hegemony. Its protection of liberal principles, combined with the residual commitment to productivity, requires a retreat from practicality.

The other side of liberalism retains the commitment to practicality by sliding toward a technocratic conception of politics. It acknowledges indirectly the dilemma of legitimacy by insisting that significant areas of social life must be regulated increasingly through an elaborate set of incentives and coercive devices. Since these controls are thought only to do more consciously and coherently what traditional guides to conduct did unconsciously and unevenly, it can be concluded that they represent no real threat to liberty or democracy. By treating, first, widespread resistance to role expectations as a universal condition, second, the ends of the civilization as inherently rational, and, third, the enlarged sphere of social life in need of conscious coordination as merely a function of the greater complexity of the system of productivity, the technocrats retain both practicality and the semblance of concern for liberal freedoms. When the order is understood in this way, it is not an unjust infringement of freedom to do what is necessary to promote rational ends.

3. A good example of this principled liberalism can be found in Ronald Dworkin, "Liberalism," in Stuart Hampshire, ed., *Public and Private Morality* (Cambridge: Cambridge University Press, 1978), pp. 113-43. The essence of liberalism, says Dworkin, is not some particular conception of the good life or commitment to some particular set of institutional practices. It is to "treat all its citizens with equal concern and respect." This principle requires government to "be neutral on what might be called the question of the good life." But to conclude that established institutions meet this requirement, Dworkin is implicitly required to narrow the variety of "conceptions of the good life" to those which fall within the range of tolerance of the established system of productivity. And if its tolerance becomes more restricted, his conceptions are likely to become more abstract. Similar tendencies can be found in George Kateb's challenging essay "On the 'Legitimation Crisis,'" cited above. Kateb wants to preserve the open, exploratory conception of self encouraged by representative democracy. (That's the interesting part.) But he thinks the concentration on "economic" issues tends to lose sight of that dimension of political life. I contend that we must politicize our understanding of economic life and seek ways to infuse these "instrumentalities" with space for the open self. Failing that, the instrumentalities are likely to overwhelm the political sphere, as that sphere is understood by the beautiful souls. To them I must appear as an ugly duckling.

Charles Schultze, the last liberal intellectual to hold a position of importance in the government, represents this perspective when he reverses the traditional rationale for the market. If it was once thought to price goods rationally, to promote personal freedom, and to limit the effective hegemony of the state, it is now to become an instrument of state control. The idea is to introduce a system of incentives into the market so that it becomes more in the self-interest of workers, owners, and consumers to promote the imperatives of the civilization of productivity. This politicization of the market will work because it does not depend upon civic resources that are in scarce supply: it "reduces the need for compassion, patriotism, brotherly love, and cultural solidarity as motivating forces behind social improvements."[4]

This particular version of the theory contains serious defects. The introduction of these incentives will merely provide new motives and possibilities for evasion, unless the purposes they serve and the sacrifices they impose speak to the convictions of large segments of the populace. They enhance the space, for instance, for the growth of the "underground economy." Failing to understand the logic of this reaction, Schultze will be drawn into a negative dialectic whereby each new set of evasions must be met by a new set of incentives and controls. The dialectic of social dissolution thus moves in tandem with a corollary dialectic of regimentation. This, then, is the version of the dilemma of legitimacy which emerges in the Schultzean theory, but it is not clearly recognized within the theory itself.

Schultze does faintly discern its outlines. For while he finds it unrealistic to promote public purposes without the institution of private incentives, he does ask how those incentives could be equitably introduced by democratic means. Confronting this issue, Schultze is forced to end "rather lamely." When we move from the regulation of private conduct to the question of forming the public will to establish those regulations, there turns out to "be no instrumental solution to the dilemma."[5] Exactly.

Schultze refuses to consider the next step. It is likely to be considered, though, by those technocrats who are no longer haunted by the ghost of liberal principles. The recent attraction of former liberals to the new theory of "reindustrialization" is one index of how far the commitment to practicality can pull many proponents away from democratic convictions as the imperatives of the civilization of productivity make them-

---

4. Charles Schultze, *The Public Use of Private Interest* (Washington, D.C.: Brookings Institution, 1977), pp. 17-18.

5. Ibid.

selves felt more powerfully.[6] The dilemma of legitimacy produces a bifurcation of contemporary liberalism. When the two sides are brought into juxtaposition, we can see the dilemma at work in the background. For either liberal practicality or the belief in liberal ideals must be sacrificed by those who refuse to reconsider the priorities and standards governing the civilization of productivity.

The Retreat of Critical Theory

The interpretation of the declining allegiance to the civilization of productivity advanced in this essay owes a considerable debt to the theories of "legitimacy" and "motivation" crisis developed by Jürgen Habermas.[7] Habermas explores the ways in which the evolution of "advanced capitalism" undermines its preconditions of healthy existence, depletes the motives needed to carry out the dictates of production, forces the state into the role of subsidizer and supporter of private production, and imposes new limits on the state's ability to meet the needs of constituencies to whom it is formally accountable.[8]

6. *Business Week* of June 30, 1980, is devoted to "The Reindustrialization of America." See Chap. 2, above.) The defining ends and promises of the civilization of productivity are there interpreted as excessive expectations on its behalf. To reindustralize, we supposedly must give up these high expectations. We must (1) shift from an emphasis on consumption to one on savings and investment; (2) shift within investment away from "quality of life improvements" toward the "production of capital goods"; (3) increase state subsidies to business; (4) form a new social contract in which workers give "management more help in improving productivity" and agree as well to decrease the rate of pay increases: (5) shift to coal and relax environmental constraints on its use; (6) introduce tax reforms to allow much higher depreciation allowances for business; (7) deregulate business to reduce impediments to growth and business costs of compliance; (8) increase military expenditures massively. With this in mind, my disagreement with the beautiful souls can be articulated more specifically. The reindustrializationists are approximately correct about what it would take to get the civilization of productivity rolling again: a progressive withdrawal from cherished liberal principles. Liberal principles are threatened if the system of productivity does not meet these imperatives, and they are threatened if it does. This "deconstruction" of the beautiful soul is designed to bring out a certain beauty in its retreat and to open it to the possibility of reconsidering its residual commitment to the civilization of productivity.

7. See Jürgen Habermas, *Legitimation Crisis* (Boston: Beacon Press, 1973). My debt to and differences from Habemas are formulated in Chap. 5, above.

8. I prefer the (no doubt awkward) term "civilization of productivity" to Habermas' "advanced capitalism" for a variety of reasons. First, it refers to the fact that existing

The theory deepens our comprehension of the problem of legitimacy in modern society. It helps us to understand why a range of practices which previously appeared to be coordinated through the impersonal market and unreflective tradition are now necessarily and visibly objects of conscious coordination by the state or private bureaucracies. Arrangements which previously appeared to be left to the market, such as income distribution, employment levels, comparative rates of development in different parts of the country, and the protection of the environment, are now the visible objects of political contestation; and those which previously appeared to be governed by unreflective tradition, such as the sexual division of labor, the treatment of old people, the composition of the school curriculum, the relations between parents and children, are now the visible objects of state policy. This means that the scope of policies and practices which must be legitimated explicitly to the citizenry has expanded. The question of legitimacy now encompasses an enlarged ensemble of social relations.

Habermas also shows us why it is no longer possible to aspire either to a democratic society in which citizens unreflectively identify with the way of life they share in common (the classic idea of civic virtue) or to one in which the citizenry has become highly privatized (the idea of civil liberty without civic virtue). Democratic politics today requires a combination of citizen self-consciousness and civic virtue. A relentless attempt to restore unreflective tradition today must issue in fascist control; and the attempt to secure democratic order without civic virtue must founder against the imperative to coordinate by conscious means a wide variety of social practices and activities. To accept these two

socialist societies are also mobilized around the priorities of economic growth, rendering them inappropriate as contrast models. Second, it signals a refusal to organize a critique around the labor theory of value, thereby rejecting the idea that one technical analysis of the order can be supplanted by another. Third, it refers to the intersubjective dimension within the modes of work, consumption, and bureaucratic control constituting the system of productivity without losing sight of the ways in which those institutions form a complex structure. Fourth, it suggests the possibility that the priorities of productivity could overwhelm the practice of democracy. The squeeze on democratic politics could occur if the priorities are not met (i.e., intensified contestation over the limited economic pie could cast the democracy of compromise and equity into disarray); and it could occur if the priorities are met (i.e., forceful imposition of sacrifices on those without strategic market or political resources could close many out of effective citizenship).

The Dilemma of Legitimacy

themes, though, is to establish both the primacy of the question of legitimacy and the difficulties in responding to it democratically.

Habermas does not seem to me to confront this last issue directly enough. Rather he acknowledges it indirectly by retreating to a meta-theoretical question. He does not ask what reforms and new priorities could hope to be instituted and to attract the reflective allegiance of the populace. He asks instead how in principle could we decide whether a particular complex of understandings and practices is valid. The current question of legitimacy is translated into a universal problem of knowledge. The consensus theory of truth and morality emerges as the answer.

The theory can be criticized, even at the abstract level at which it is pitched. (See Chap. 5.) The problem is that the expressive theory of language and discourse Habermas draws upon to construct his ideal of pure discourse contains within it the expectation that a discourse is unlikely to achieve the practical consensus to which Habermas aspires. Any consensus capable of generating specific courses of action will be based upon some set of prejudgments which cannot be called into question during that discourse. Some set of prejudgments must form the unreflective background of discourse while others are called into question, or the discourse will lack sufficient density to generate a conclusion. And if inquiry into a broader range of prejudgments is encouraged, no free consensus is likely to emerge.

There is something apolitical in this ideal of a perfect consensus, even if it is situated outside the realm of historical probability. It understates the extent to which our limited resources of reason and evidence unavoidably generate a plurality of reasonable answers to perplexing practical questions. It thus fails to appreciate the creative role for politics in those persisting situations where public action must be taken and the resources of knowledge are insufficient to generate a single result. As an ideal, it aspires to take the heat out of the cauldron of contested interpretations and orientations to action. It is in this sense closer to a collectivization of administration than to the democratization of politics. In asking too much for legitimacy, it takes too much away from politics.

Yet apprehended from another angle, the construction of the ideal speech situation (and other versions of the consensus theory of practical judgment) can be seen to carry a political message. It is a symbol as well as a construct. It expresses the anxiety that the potential dilemma of legitimacy actually may be realized in history. It conveys the fear that the space for democratic discourse may become squeezed increasingly by the imperatives of the political economy. As a "limiting case," unintended for full achievement, it helps to insulate thought from a world which threatens to become less hospitable to democratic ideals; it is an intellectual retreat which protects the idea of democracy by placing it beyond the reach of practical imperatives. The Habermas doctrine, failing as a theory of truth, succeeds as a symbol of the dilemma of legitimacy.

The Foucauldian Reversal

Foucault would be unsurprised by the critique of the discourse theory of truth briefly outlined here. It is authorized by the "episteme" governing modern discourse.[9] Whether defined as the implicit, the unconscious, the sedimented, the in-itself, the horizon, or the intersubjective background, theoretical discourse since the nineteenth century has been haunted by the unthought which provides the ground for its vaunted celebration of reflexivity or self-consciousness. Every philosophy which celebrates reflexivity also makes the material it works upon recede constantly into the darkness. Modern "man" (as Foucault describes us) is endlessly pursued by a "double," by "the other that is not only a brother, but a twin," by an unshakable shadow "both exterior to him and indispensable to him."[10]

This eternal regress in the relation between the thought and the unthought, between the subject and its other, makes reflexivity possible at the expense of rendering a valid political consensus impossible. It is

9. An episteme does not produce the hegemony of one discourse (ideology) over all others; it does produce the space in which alternative discourses can function. The episteme enables and confines theoretical discourse. It renders inoperative today, for instance, the theory of words as signs residing within the world conveying an etenal meaning to be interpreted by commentators; and it thereby renders the Renaissance comprehension of madness as a meaningful text to be deciphered inoperative. A "discursive practice" functions inside the space provided by the episteme; it is a set of concepts, instruments, architectural structures, regulations, credentials, and rules of evidence which operate at a practical level. Penology and psychiatry are operative disciplines; prisons and asylums are among the media in which they function; delinquents, criminals, and a variety of mental patients are the objects they constitute and treat. These elements together form the discursive practices of criminology and psychiatry. The modern episteme allows these, but it does not uniquely determine them. It forecloses punishment as spectacle, for instance, because we cannot now think of the torture-confession complex as a sign of truth; but it allows the juridical conception of crime (rational agents who are responsible and guilty) to function alongside the treatment model. The shift in emphasis in the Foucauldian texts from archeology to genealogy would need to be treated in a thorough discussion of his thought. I will not attempt that here.

10. *The Order of Things* (New York: Random House, 1970), p. 326.

The Dilemma of Legitimacy

always possible to dissent from any new interpretation of the previously unthought. "For modern thought, no morality is possible. . . . As soon as [thought] functions it offends or reconciles, attracts or repels, breaks, dissociates, unites or reunites; it cannot help but liberate and enslave."[11] My critique of Habermas, then, operates within the episteme which authorizes it. But it does not, Foucault would insist, pursue its own line to the limits. It fails to enunciate how the very problematic of legitimacy, with its associated concepts of the subject, freedom, reflexivity, allegiance, responsibility, and consent, is the juridical twin of the problematic of disciplinary order. The former is not, as it sees itself, the alternative to the latter; the two function together to produce the modern subject and to subject it to the dictates of the order. The critique, in Foucauldian terms, sets the stage for the reversal of the problematic of legitimacy.

In a perfectly legitimate order, the imperative becomes the indicative: the "you must" assumes the form of "we will." All seems smooth and unruffled, but the voice of the body can still be detected beneath the whine of the socially produced soul. To extrapolate slightly, we might apply Foucault's documentary studies to an account of the relation between the theoretical perspectives of Jean-Jacques Rousseau and the marquis de Sade. For Sade is not merely the adversary of Rousseau; the theorist of illicit desire is the double of the theorist of civic virtue. Rousseau's legitimate order invokes the free acceptance of self-restraint, the communal endorsement of self-censorship, the production of chaste, subordinate women. And the Sadean counterorder, perfect in its own way, treats these limits as invitations to transgressions: restraints are produced to be broken; censorship intensifies the will to pornography; and the women of virture become the perfect objects of degradation.

By demanding self-restraint in pursuit of virtue, Rousseau's polity loads the counterself with illicit desires. It doubles pleasure by adding the pleasure of transgression to the original desire, and the world of virtue produces perfect human objects for the realization of its intensified pleasures. Rousseau's vision of order through virtue thus contains virtue and an underground world of illicit desire. He articulates one side of this polity, and Sade articulates the other. Without the presence of the other to oppose and to provide the contrast against which virtue is defined, virtue could not emerge as an achievement; without the other embodied in specific figures of vice, virtue could not fend off the other in itself. But an order which constitutes vice in this way assures that the other will appear in a more aggressive form: it appears

11. Ibid., p. 328.

as those who take special pleasure in violating virtue. The struggle between vice and virtue is thus loaded in favor of vice, and the virtuous order thereby generates internal pressures to convert the other from the classical figure of vice into the modern object of medical treatment. The classical idea (or this version of it) sets up the modern order which medicalizes insanity, delinquency, sexual perversity, and abnormality. The new order subjects these newly defined figures to treatment; it strives thereby to dampen the pleasures that classical vice had experienced in its struggle with virtue. The old ideal prepares us for modern modes of treatment and discipline.

Individualization is the process by which the modern disciplinary self is produced. One part of the self endorses the rules of the order; it is the free, rational, responsible agent, worthy of punishment for breaking norms to which it freely consents. The second part represents the other which individuals seek to expunge in themselves and to treat when others manifest it in criminality, delinquency, madness, or perverse sexuality. The juridical apparatus and the disciplinary apparatus together constitute the subject and its other.

> In a system of discipline, the child is more individualized than the adult, the patient more than the healthy man, the madman and the delinquent more than the normal and non-delinquent. In each case, it is towards the first of these pairs that all the individualizing mechanisms are turned in our civilization; and when one wishes to individualize the healthy, moral and law-abiding adult, it is always by asking how much of the child he has in him, what fundamental crime he has dreamt of committing. . . . All the sciences, analyses or practices employing the root "psycho-" have their origin in this historical reversal of the procedures of individualization.[12]

Foucault's texts seek to document the multiple ways in which modern attempts to liberate sexuality, madness, and criminality from arbitrary and repressive controls entangle the self in a web of more insidious controls. The politics of liberation, in its radical and liberal guises, actually helps to produce the subject and to subjugate those other parts of the self which do not fit into this production. The reforms typically medicalize sexuality, delinquency, mental "illness." They enclose the objects of treatment in a web of "insidious leniencies."

12. Michel Foucault, *Discipline and Punish*, trans. Alan Sheridan (New York: Random House, 1977), p. 193.

Critical legitimists, of whom I am one, are generally eager to shrug off Foucault. We seek not to subjugate people in this order, but to imagine a counterorder which is worthy of their allegiance. But Foucault seems to identify us with our adversaries, and that could not be quite right. Besides, his vocabulary is inflated, and we speak more carefully.

But I do not think we (I) can be let off the hook so easily. Foucault's detailed archeologies remind us how the dictates of a particular order and the conceptual resources of a particular episteme can soon appear barbaric to its successor (e.g., the way the ships of fools and torture as instruments of truth appear to us today). The history of unreason indirectly challenges the contemporary constitution of reason. Moreover, if Foucault's metaphors seem inflated to us, they challenge us to justify the mellow metaphors through which we characterize either the existing order or the one we would bring into being. In substituting "surveillance" for "observation," "interrogate" for "question," "interrupt" for "pause," and "production" for "emergence" (in talking about the "origin" of the self), he at once challenges the transparency of the mellow metaphors we adopt and claims to detect hidden violence within the discourse of the legitimist. In elaborating the microphysics of the modern subject as a disciplinary production, he is unmasking the denial of the body and how that denial functions. Legitimists are treated as participants in the cover-up. Our metaphors, slipped silently into our discourse, provide the medium through which our potential violence is disguised.

After Foucault, we can understand more clearly why Habermas struggled so valiantly to validate the principle of a free and rational consensus. For that would be a consensus which did not enslave while it liberated; it would create unity without subjugating the other. We can also understand why Foucault must read the project as a counter-tyranny of insidious leniency. For it constantly insists on assimilating material into its categories which can be made to fit only by force. It practices denial in the name of free discourse.

The case can be made, I think, that the legitimist, particularly the dissident type, should accept Foucault as a double. The quest for legitimacy must open itself to the voice of the other; it must review itself from the vantage point of conceptualizations it finds alien, questions it tends to ignore, and answers it tends to exclude. It must confront three questions. What is to be done to, with, or "for" the other which does not fit into the actual or ideal order? What is the justification for doing it? And what is the ground of the justification?

But can Foucault demand more? Must the quest for legitimacy itself be expunged because *any* answer given to it must tyrannize and subjugate? I think not. For Foucault is entangled in his own version of the dilemma of legitimacy. Consider the political strategy open to Foucault after the strategies of technocratic control, liberal reform, and radical liberation have been rejected. In his early work, Foucault sought to allow the "voice of unreason" to speak for itself by historicizing the various relations to the other imposed by historical variations in the constitution of reason. His more recent stance is more overtly political; he now supports "the insurrection of subjugated knowledges," and he is now more confident in his belief that the attempt to "understand" the other within any established framework amounts to the attempt to control the other by insidious leniency.[13]

Yet Foucault is not, as he would characterize it, a naive anarchist of the nineteenth century. He does not seem to believe that an anarchistic order could be established. Order is unavoidable for social life; and any order, particularly any order in the modern world, necessarily implies limits.[14] Thus to oppose in principle the quest for legitimacy is to deny one postulate in the Foucauldian problematic. It is to subjugate one dimension of Foucauldian thought in the interest (the political interest) of allowing the other dimension to flourish. "To imagine another system," Foucault contends, "is to extend our participation in the present system . . . ; the 'whole of society' is precisely that which should not be considered except as something to be destroyed."[15]

But if I am right, the exclusion of political affirmation emerges as the Foucauldian denial. Strategic considerations lead him to mask a dimension of his own theory, and the denial is fraught with dangerous consequences. The release of subjugated knowledges may illuminate political imagination, but the need remains to establish a stance, even if

13. Michel Foucault, *Power/Knowledge* (Brighton, Sussex: Harvester Press, 1980), p. 81. My reading of the earlier texts is supported by this more recent essay: "it is not through recourse to sovereignty against discipline that the effects of disciplinary power can be limited because sovereignty and disciplinary mechanisms are two absolutely integral constituents of the general mechanisms of power in our society" (p. 108).

14. Another defense of Foucauldian strategy rests upon the view that, since the forces of order are always with us, we need a counterforce unconfined by the need to affirm and, thereby, unconfined by the need to limit itself. But a reversal of the reversal is needed here: since the voice of order is always with us, we need to legitimize oppositional efforts through counteraffirmations to gain leverage.

15. *Language, Counter-memory, Practice* (Oxford: Basil Blackwell, 1977), pp. 230, 233. Since this essay was written, in 1980, Foucault has affirmed a conception of self as a work of art. And there are hints as well about a vision of society where "normalization" is reduced. But these hints are not articulated as a political vision; their development would require him to transcend his favorite stance—that of the modern fool.

The Dilemma of Legitimacy

it is an ambiguous one, toward those limits most deserving of allegiance.

The dilemma of legitimacy inside Foucault's theory thus emerges
starkly. It becomes a dilemma of order: social life requires order, but the
order which does receive the allegiance of its subjects subjugates them,
while the one which does not subjugates them too.[16]

The way to loosen the hold of this dilemma, at least at the level of
theory, is to show that the circle of reflexivity is not as closed as Foucault
pretends it must be. We may concede that the assimilation of the other to
established dualities of reason/unreason, virtue/vice, sanity/insanity,
and normality/abnormality always contains the elements of a political
conquest. For Foucault's documentary histories do support the conclusion that standards and judgments which possessed hegemony at one
historic moment appear arbitrary and closed from the perspective of
another; and we can therefore suspect that those categories which now
govern our thought and practice will assume such an appearance at a
later date. Thus the view of reflexivity which assumes that we can listen
to the other through our categories or that we can now broaden them
enough to draw the other into their orbit without arbitrariness must now
appear to be too narrow; the circle in which it moves is too tightly
drawn. But what about a mode of reflexivity which profits from
Foucault's histories of madness, criminality, and perversity and which
acknowledges that it now lacks the resources to comprehend the other?
What about a mode which reflexively acknowledges the limits to reflexive assimilation of the other? Such a view warrants a different response:
it encourages us to find space for the other to live and speak on the
ground that we know enough to know that we cannot comprehend it.
It supports, I want to say, an ideal of social order which can sustain itself without having to draw so much of the self into the orbit of social
control.

This theoretic response contains implications for political conduct. If
ours is an order with "dirt-denying" tendencies; if we tend to sweep
that which is out of place under the rug by pretending that we can
assimilate it to established categories of rationality and treatment; if we
medicalize, confine, and exclude the others who do not fit into the existing order of things: there have been other societies with a loose enough
texture to be more "dirt affirming."[17] They could acknowledge the dirt

16. In *Power/Knowledge*, Foucault declares: "Right should be viewed, I believe, not in
terms of a legitimacy to be established, but in terms of the methods of subjugation it
instigates" (p. 96).

17. The terms are borrowed from Mary Douglas (who borrowed them from William
James). See *Purity and Danger* (Baltimore: Penguin Books, 1966).

that they themselves produced and thereby (though imperfectly or ambiguously) confront the limits of their own conceptual and political orders.

Tribal festivals of reversal had this quality. Seasonal festivals were enacted in which that which was forbidden was allowed and those who were normally subordinated (because their order necessitated it) were temporarily placed in a superior position. In these festivals, that which was officially circumscribed or denied was temporarily allowed and affirmed. The participants were able to glimpse the injustices implicit in their own necessities; they were encouraged to live these necessities with more humanity during the normal periods of the year. They acknowledged that some features of their own order, some of the dirt they produced, was mysterious to them. The reins of social coordination were not so tightly drawn that they had to pretend that they possessed sufficient categories to comprehend and eliminate the dirt in their order.

One criterion of comparative legitimacy suggested by the Foucauldian forays into the logic of unreason speaks to the differential capacity of regimes to acknowledge the dirt, the matter out of place, they themselves produce. The civilization of productivity, if its actual trajectory fits the course projected earlier in this essay, will be too constrained by the drive to mobilize its populace around the simultaneous pursuit of growth and austerity to nourish this capacity. To challenge the interdependent complexes of consumption, production, profit, and resource dependency which generate these imperatives is thus to challenge the preconditions of closure in the order. A margin of success on this terrain could help to maintain space for political dialogue. If, for instance, the infrastructure of consumption were reconstituted so that the intensification of consumption demands (or pleas) was not fueled by the perpetual expansion of consumption needs, the imperative to impose growth and austerity together could be relaxed.[18] The effect would be the provision of needed slack in the order, allowing political engage-

---

18. To change the infrastructure of consumption, it is necessary to revise also the modes of investment, profit, work, and state expenditures. These themes are developed in Best and Connolly, *The Politicized Economy*. I think the alternatives reduce to three: (1) refusing to support the imperatives of the system of productivity without modifying the institutions which produce them; (2) successfully imposing austerity on politically weakened constituencies to provide the basis for "reindustrialization"; (3) reconstituting the established mode of consumption, etc., to curtail imperatives. Each of these strategies would face resistance, opposition, limits, setbacks, and so forth. But only one of them contains the promise to preserve space for democratic politics. That is also the one (3) which is unexplored within the established terms of political discourse.

The Dilemma of Legitimacy

ment to be the medium through which we probe the ambiguities and cope with the limits of modern social life.

By "slack in the order," I mean an order which does not have to coordinate so many aspects of our lives and relations to maintain itself; an order which can afford to let some forms of conduct be; an order which is not compelled by its own imperatives of coordination to convert eccentric, odd, strange behavior into the categories of vice, delinquency, or abnormality. Such an order would require virtue among its citizens, but the space virtue must cover would not extend too broadly; a residual space would flourish in which neither the control of virtue nor coercion would be necessary. The provision of that space would itself allow virtue to displace coercive discipline in those areas where the order did require coordination to sustain itself.

This, at least, is the vision which seems to me to contain the most promise for responding to the dilemma of legitimacy. But slack in the order can be produced only if we can find ways to tame or relax the new imperatives which are generated by the civilization of productivity. And (again I express only an intuition) the relaxation of those imperatives can best be achieved if we reconstitute the infrastructure of consumption to reduce those consumption needs which now impel citizens to validate through the political process social disciplines and sacrifice which they themselves find onerous.

Perhaps there are other or better ways to promote slack in the order, but here I want to concentrate on the importance of the end rather than on the most appropriate means to it. For when the legitimist introduces the conception of slack into the problematic of legitimacy, we can hear the echo of an earlier liberal doctrine in the background. A theory which has been inspired by the wish to leave liberal notions of privacy, rights, tolerance, and diversity behind now redefines and reinstitutes them. The irony in this new vision contains the seeds of a renewed dialogue between liberals and radicals. For although the liberal appreciation of private space is acknowledged in this vision, it sees that established liberal programs and priorities now erode both that space and the implicit allegiance of the populace to the order. Similarly, the radical appreciation of virtue is now endorsed as well as the understanding that an order must produce a double dialectic of regimentation and corruption when it loses the ability to sustain the affective allegiance of its participants. But the radical image is then modified by the admission that the ideal of virtue and legitimacy requires the provision of slack in the order. Slack is both a precondition of and limit to virtue in a modern polity.

Resentment and Legitimacy

We are now in a position to identify another element in the dilemma of legitimacy stalking the civilization of productivity. Why, it might be asked, is there so much resentment expressed in contemporary politics? Whites against blacks, men against women, straights against gays, workers against welfare recipients, the old against the young, and, in each case, the reverse as well. We have explained one of its dimensions by showing how the claims of some of these groups invalidate the dignity and identity available to others. But a second dimension enters into this politics of resentment as well.

The American dream is too pure for this world. Its definition lacks an appreciation of the dirt and ambiguity lodged in any ideal, and so even its attainment fosters resentment: resentment against the life actually available to those who receive its paradigmatic rewards. This dimension of resentment makes privileged beneficiaries and their satellites resistant to sacrifices that might enable others to be drawn into the circle of privilege. Thus the resentment of the white working class contains two interwoven dimensions: they resent being asked to sacrifice for those below them when their own experience of the good life available seems so marginal and precarious, and they resent those above them who react to ambiguities contained within the most fulsome experience of that life. A dialectic of resentment haunts the pursuit of the good life in America. It is determined partly by self-defeating elements in the very conception of the good life and partly by the insistence that any good life pursued be free of dirt in its essence.

The most stubborn element in the modern experience of disaffection is the refusal to affirm ambiguities within standards and achievements most worthy of endorsement, ambiguities lodged, for example, in the identity of the self as a subject, in democracy as the essence of the common good, in standards of justice worthy of respect. It is this element in the politics of resentment that I seek to interrogate further. What is involved in the insistence to posit ideals without dirt? What are the relations between the intolerance of ambiguity and the all too ready tolerance of discipline imposed on the "other" in contemporary life? How can we come to appreciate ambiguities while affirming ends worthy of endorsement?

The intuition guiding this exploration is a simple one: until the contemporary self is prepared to affirm ambiguities in ideals it prizes most, it will oscillate between cultivating innocence about the historical

The Dilemma of Legitimacy

course we are on and expressing covert disaffection from it. Both responses, when transmuted into politics, license extension of disciplinary controls into new areas of life.

7

DISCIPLINE, POLITICS,

AMBIGUITY

Unconscious Contrivances of Control

Is there a sense in which liberal and radical thought together obscure modes of disciplinary control in modernity? A sense, that is, in which the conceptions of self held by radical proponents of civic virtue and liberal defenders of human interests and rights combine to conceal the violence required to produce and maintain the modern self? Michel Foucault thinks there is. He treats liberalism and radicalism as two complementary doctrines; together they enter into those discursive practices which constitute "disciplinary society."

I will explore this question, first, by offering a brief account of contemporary modes of disciplinary control, which, though surely contestable, coheres with a conception of self common to liberals and radicals; second, by presenting the Foucauldian case for extension of the account into new corners of institutional life; and third, by responding to the Foucauldian reading with one that both profits and deviates from it. The dialectic to be pursued expresses the conviction that liberal and radical doctrines are most in need of redefinition at those obscure junctures where their differences merge into commonalities.

In an era characterized by doctrines of "reindustrialization," "supply-side economics," "rational choice," "incentive systems," "zero-sum economics," and "legitimacy deficits" a broad doctrinal drift toward the problem of managing, regulating, and controlling the behavior of people and institutions can be discerned. The liberal drive to devise means to coordinate more aspects of public and private life indeed meshes with the radical understanding that operative citizen allegiance to the roles and ends of the political economy is weak. The drive to extend discipline over those who do not discipline themselves—discernible in the programs of liberal econonmists such as Charles Schultze and Lester Thurow—represents an effort to close the gap between the imperatives of social coordination built into the political economy and the disposition of workers, owners, welfare dependents, taxpayers, children, and parents to evade, elude, resist, and oppose those imperatives.[1]

The pressures to extend disciplinary control are perhaps most prominent in the doctrine of "reindustrialization"—a loose constellation of policies and proposals designed to foster capital accumulation, deregulate business, foster worker productivity, impose austerity on low-income households, and restore rapid economic growth. Within it is discernible the drift toward militarization of welfare as young clients are told they can get the job experience they need in the army, navy, air force, and marines, and as students, facing cutbacks in civilian funds for higher education, are informed of the expansion of ROTC scholarships committing them to future military duty. Welfare is thus shifted into a bureaucracy that renders its beneficiaries more susceptible to disciplinary control. There is the corollary shift from public welfare to private philanthropy, allowing private patrons to set the terms of aid away from the glare of public accountability; the use of inflation to force those workers without effective bargaining power to accept real reductions in income; the relaxation of restrictions on domestic state surveillance; the intimidation of public- and some private-sector unions; the rapid growth of private security systems to monitor workers and consumers; the visible acts of police brutality against isolated members of the underclass; the hardening line against blue-collar crime; the campaigns to censor library books and regulate school curricula; the effort to isolate decaying cities in the Northeast and Midwest from a political coalition large enough to govern the nation; the tax revolts that eventually provoke governmental cutbacks in the budget for civilian welfare and services.

But these visible modes of control are limited in effectiveness unless they are complemented by what we might describe as unconscious contrivances of social discipline. The latter emerge when allegiance to the purposes and priorities of the political economy is low among particular constituencies, the demands for central coordination remain high, and

---

1. See Charles Schultze, *The Public Use of Private Interest* (Washington, D.C.: Brookings Institution, 1977) and Lester Thurow, *The Zero-Sum Society* (New York: Basic Books, 1980). I agree that these two texts do not exhaust the range of ideas located today under the umbrella "liberalism." But they do represent a powerful strand of liberal thought when it turns its attention to the political economy. And, I would argue, those liberals who focus on the doctrine of rights either appeal covertly to such an economic doctrine to provide the state with the dividend needed to fund welfare and protect rights, or retreat to an abstract doctrine of rights, which becomes more and more detached from the actual life of its day. I have developed the latter arguments in *Appearance and Reality in Politics* (Cambridge: Cambridge University Press, 1981), chaps. 4 and 6.

opportunities to elude or evade sacrifices and obligations imposed by private and public authorities are relatively plentiful.

Consider, by way of example, the illegal alien. Castigated by many as a thief of American jobs, the alien is a valuable commodity to labor-intensive businesses. Because the alien is illegal, he or she is a possessor of labor power without political rights. The alien is thus in a weak position to complain about wages or working conditions, to establish roots in the broader community, to organize collectively, or to participate in the political life of the society. Illegality in this instance depoliticizes; it subjects the alien to a self-imposed discipline and silence designed to shield him from the eye of the public authorities. The anonymous presence of the alien further inhibits the demands citizen workers make; and it reminds marginal citizens that they could become aliens in their own country if they step too far outside the accepted bounds of political propriety. There is thus reason in the hostility many marginal workers feel toward the alien; he both poses a threat to them and symbolizes starkly a condition they experience darkly and imperfectly. The drive of the marginal worker/citizen to maintain psychological distance from the alien contains the fear that the actual condition of the one group is too close for comfort to the possible status of the other.

Consider, to bring things closer to home, the citizen who is also a tax evader. In the 1981 Federal Income Tax Form the taxpayer is instructed to report all earnings, including "bartering income (fair market value of goods and services you returned in return for your services) . . . business expense reimbursements that cover more than you spent for those services . . . gains from the sale of . . . securities, coins, gold, silver or other property, gambling winnings, embezzled or other illegal income." The formal rules of tax payment, the difficulties of enforcement, and the intimate connection between disposable income and participation in the good life available in America combine to convert a large percentage of American citizens into low-grade criminals. A nation of tax evaders is a nation of people who, to varying degrees, have an incentive to keep a low public profile, to keep their visible life unexceptionable so that nothing unusual will excite the interest of the Internal Revenue Service or the citizens who are invited to report suspicious behavior to it.

The alien and the tax evader, as agents of self-discipline and self-depoliticization, are threads woven into the fabric of the political economy. Large sections of the political economy are woven from the same spool. The army recruit who learns to "beat the system" by seeking anonymity within it unwittingly provides support for the military as an order sustained by anonymous role bearers. The welfare freeloader, the small-time participant in the underground economy, the gambler, the drug user or dealer, the street person, the sexually perverse, the draft or draft-registration evader, the divorcee striving to retain child custody or evade child support, the informant seeking protection from organized crime, the academic researcher adapting to stringent criteria for grant support, the hooker, the professional adjusting to narrow standards for career advancement in a tight economy, the employee who has falsified educational credentials or a police record or an official history of mental instability to get a job, the alcoholic, the public official on the take—all these people, when the appropriate background conditions are operative, are drawn into the web of social control through the self-pursuit of anonymity and conventionality. Some of them literally become resident aliens, while others merely maintain a low profile to hook into the regular or irregular economy.

In each of these cases the evasion of laws or social norms in one respect operates to discipline the self in others; those who, from need or ambition, rip off the system in one way strip from themselves as well a measure of freedom and effective citizenship.

Certain attributes of these unconscious contrivances of social control need attention. First, these artifices of self-discipline are unplanned. They emerge initially as a miscellany of dispersed tactics to evade official laws and regulations. They then function as unorganized modes of social control whenever the primary strategies of control are tightly enforced; and some of them eventually become deployed as conscious instruments of control by public and private authorities. The ambiguous relation between the state and the citizen/taxpayer exemplifies this pattern of development. Individual members of the underclass, for instance, develop multiple strategies to evade payments to the state. As the phenomenon spreads it functions to reduce total revenue available to the state *and* to depoliticize the evaders. Finally, particular authorities realize that they can use the veiled threat of tightened enforcement to keep these potential elements of disruption in line.

Second, these unconscious contrivances do not function well as modes of social control during periods of prosperity and tolerance for social diversity. They solidify when the reins of conscious social coordination are drawn more tightly. Thus gays may participate openly in the life of the community until public knowledge of their sexual orientation threatens their livelihoods or community status; then they must either go underground or accept the prospect of a marginal status. Academic grantspersons can maintain congruence between their own standards and the criteria of granting agencies as long as the latter appreciate diversity in research orientation, but when the criteria are narrowly defined they must either drop out of the race or adapt their orientation to officially prescribed standards.

Third, though these mechanisms, in cumulative effect, help to displace political articulation of disaffection, they do not normally help the political economy to function efficiently. These are contrivances of order rather than efficiency, of discipline rather than state revenue, of depoliticization rather than realization of a good life shared by citizens in common. These unconscious contrivances of order proliferate when operative allegiance to role assignments is low, when belief in the future promised by the civilization of productivity has been suspended, and when no insurgent movement has crystallized to articulate the deeper discontents of disaffected constituencies. The gap opened between the order's expanded need for the coordination of individual conduct and the contracted civic virtue among subordinate sections of the populace is filled, though imperfectly and ambiguously, by these unconscious contrivances of social discipline. The mechanisms of social discipline are thus extended in tandem with the extension of social disaffection. And the dimensions of these practices that help to maintain overt social peace also support economic deterioration.

Discipline and Subjectivity

Foucault, the consummate theorist of modernity as disciplinary society, would detect major defects in the foregoing account. The conceptions of self and rationality it presupposes prohibit it from probing the mechanisms that generate the particular structures of self, rationality, virtue, sexuality, criminality, and madness appropriate to modernity. And it seems to endorse, in its opposition to the incentive systems and police powers of the present, an ideal of collectivity in which people freely identify with the ends and norms of their way of life. Its basic flaw resides in its insistence on treating an effect of disciplinary society—the unified subject as a bearer of rights, interests, and virtues—as an epistemically privileged center to be protected from repression or unjust coercion. The account thus perceives disciplines that limit the subject but not those that constitute the subject, and it misses these latter pressures because it insists on construing the unified subject as a rational achievement of modernity.

Modernity, on Foucault's reading, is sustained by drawing the self systematically into the orbit of social discipline. It is not coincidental that paranoia—the constant sense of being under surveillance by others—is the paradigmatic mental illness of modernity. For the politics of control through visibility of the self to agents of normalization encourages self-protection of one's status as a free, responsible agent through self-containment of impulses and inclinations that do not conform to established standards of normality. The normalized self is, for Foucault, the self that maintains self-surveillance to avoid treatment for delinquency, mental illness, or sexual perversity; disciplinary society *is* the order that extends strategies of normalization into new frontiers of social life. The humanist critics of repressive politics and the overt agents of coercive control are, on this reading, Siamese twins. Facing in different directions, they are bound together at the back; strategies of normalization pursued by the advocates of civic virtue, sexual liberation, client-centered therapy, and prison reform complement the overt forms of coercion pursued by police and intelligence bureaucracies as well as the incentive systems forged by policy scientists. As Foucault's genealogies of madness, therapy, medicine, crime, and sexuality are designed to show, these twin strategies function together (behind the backs of the intellectuals who constitute them as oppositional) to extend the tentacles of order more deeply into the self.

The logic of Foucault's account is exhibited in his history of madness.[2] The literature and art of the late Middle Ages were preoccupied with folly. Lodged within a world alive with the signs of God's purpose and will, folly signified a self both fallen from humanity and possessed by a truth beyond the powers of human articulation. Since the phenomenon was suspended in ambiguity, the social response to madness was ambiguous. It was simultaneously an object of fear and fascination, a danger to be avoided and a dark sign to be read for clues about the human condition and its relation to the larger cosmos. The Ship of Fools, a symbol of significance beyond its actual use, embodied this ambiguity. On these ships the mad were at once separated from society and free to travel on water in pursuit of their lost humanity; they could seek purification on the waterways and provide ordinary people, when the ships pulled into the harbor, with glimpses into the mysteries of human life and the limits of human reason.

> What does it presage, this wisdom of fools? Doubtless since it is
> a forbidden wisdom, it presages both the reign of Satan and the
> end of the world; ultimate bliss and supreme punishment;

2. There have been notable shifts in Foucault's theory between the early work exemplified by *Madness and Civilization* (New York: Random House, 1965) and the later position represented by *Discipline and Punish* (New York: Pantheon, 1977) and *The History of Sexuality* (New York: Vintage Press, 1980), but my point now is to delineate common themes that cut across these divisions.

omnipotence on earth and the infernal fall. The Ship of Fools sails through a landscape of delights, where all is offered to desire, a sort of renewed paradise, since there no man knows either suffering or need; and yet has not recovered his innocence. . . . When man deploys the arbitrary nature of his madness he confronts the dark necessity of the world; the animal that haunts his nightmares and his nights of privation in his own nature, which will lay bare hell's pitiless truth.[3]

But modernity, through a series of stages launched during the Enlightenment, has squeezed the ambiguity out of madness. Madness is now constituted as unreason, and the processes by which we confine, exclude, medicalize, and cure it ensure that reason, in its modern guise, can avoid awareness of limits or antinomies it may contain. The agents of control and confinement unite with their unwitting allies, the agents of rehabilitation and treatment, to define the mad as victims of a disease to be cured or controlled, never as *signs* that the norms from which they deviate are too demanding or destructive of the self to which they are applied. The occurrence of mental illness, in the modern era of persons, freedom, and responsibility, authorizes officials to suspend rights to self-control; and the knowledge that such a suspension might be invoked encourages one to contain those aspects of self that do not fit into established standards. Madness is, on the Foucauldian reading, a real phenomenon, and its bearers do suffer immensely. But its modern mode functions politically to ward off deconstructions of established standards of reason and normality and to establish the modern self as a locus of disciplinary normalization.

A corollary shift occurs in the modern orientation to criminality. In late medieval Europe torture was a closely regulated means of discovering the truth of crime, and punishment was a public spectacle through which the sovereign displayed his power and vengeance to the assembled crowd. The spectacle expressed a certain ambiguity; for here the crowd might listen to the condemned man denounce the sovereign, and here on occasion the crowd might support the condemned against the sovereign. The political dimension of crime—its ambiguous embodiment of avarice and opposition to the order—could emerge in these spectacles. People could glimpse arbitrary elements in their own order through the spectacle of crime and punishment.

But here too ambiguity has now been subdued. The criminal is either a person who has voluntarily broken a just code to which he had pre-

---

3. Foucault, *Madness and Civilization*, pp. 22-23.

viously consented or a delinquent who has lost self-control. He is either an agent to be punished or the bearer of an illness to be treated.

It is well known that modern prisons breed hardened criminals. That effect, Foucault insists, is not one of its failures but the sign of its greatest success. Modern penality depoliticizes crime; it draws attention to the character of the criminal and away from the power of the regime; and it separates the criminal from other disaffected elements of the population. The spread of crime thus seldom jeopardizes the order. Rather it constantly renews the cry for law and order or, when that cycle has exhausted itself, for the rehabilitation of delinquents. In either event, the contemporary constitution of crime fosters the perfection and extension of techniques for surveillance, treatment, and coercive control, which increasingly typify disciplinary society. To use a non-Foucaultian vocabulary, the range of legitimate political issues is constricted by these social disciplines even while the formal channels of democratic politics remain open.

These shifts in the constitution of madness and criminality, along with a corollary series of shifts in the organization of medicine, sexuality, and education, correlate with the persistent drift of modernity toward a more tightly articulated order. The emergence of modern practices of bureaucratic control, market discipline, therapeutic help, democratic virtue, and sexual liberation, though each often defines itself in opposition to others, meshes with the global tendency of modern orders to organize the self into an agent of self-containment. Neither Rousseau nor Hobbes, Bentham nor Locke, Marx nor Hegel, has understood the dynamics of this process in all its complexity. Each in opposing the others has obscured the ways in which his own ideals anticipate some dimension of disciplinary society.

Disciplinary society is perpetuated through the production and deployment of the bifurcated self, while public life pulsates with debates over which side of this bifurcation should receive priority in the treatment of crime, perversity, welfare cheating, and personal instability. One side of the self—the site of the free, self-interested, rational, and responsible agent—endorses the norms of the order as its own postulates of reason and morality; it contains those aspects of the self that do not correspond to these constructions; and when it breaks one of the codes to which it has consented, it is worthy of being held responsible for the infringement. The second side is "the other" in the self, which does not fit neatly into this affirmative construction; it is the locus of wishes, feelings, and desires that escape articulation. To give these impulses verbal expression today is to translate them into the language of therapy, medicine, psychiatry, and moral perversity. This other side of the self is also a site of political control; for behavior that escapes the self-control of reason, interest, and responsibility is located within categories that require bureaucratic intervention to control, reform, or prevent it.

The bifurcated self of modernity, then, is susceptible to multiple strategies of discipline; each side is penetrated by social discipline; and the side receiving the most attention in a particular case is the one that appears most vulnerable to available tactics of control. That is why Foucault can contend that modern "individualization" is really a complex set of processes by which the bifurcated self is produced. Its behavior is recorded in "individualized" files, and its conduct is normalized through a heterogeneous ensemble of disciplinary tactics. Bureaucratization and individualization, incentive systems governing self-interested agents, and moral codes internalized by virtuous citizens are, on this reading, complementary mechanisms of disciplinary control.

Self-Reflexivity and Ambiguity

This is an incomplete account of Foucault's picture of disciplinary society and the modern self. It ignores, for instance, counterpressures spawned within those parts of the self (and especially those selves defined as others) which resist these mechanisms of normalization and subjectification. It will suffice to allow us to pose some pertinent issues about the alternatives to disciplinary politics; for when modernity is characterized in this way it appears that we must either give up any aspiration to a society in which democracy flourishes or reject this entire archeology of disciplinary society. We can be democrats or nihilists; we can criticize the present from the perspective of alternative ideals or join Foucault in repudiating every ideal imaginable today as the tyrannical extension of "our participation in the present system."[4]

But perhaps these options have been posed too starkly by both Foucault and his humanist adversaries. It may be possible to articulate a vision of democratic life that consciously maintains tension between these two tendencies, affirming the legitimacy of limits and conventions essential to democratic politics while otherwise exposing and opposing the modern drift toward rationalization, normalization, and dependency. Acknowledging intractable points of opposition between the

4. *Language, Counter-memory, Practice* (Oxford: Basil Blackwell, 1977), p. 230.

Discipline, Politics, Ambiguity

drive to disturb forces of normalization and the quest to sustain precon-ditions of democratic life, it might show how each, properly under-stood, is a precondition and a limit to the other. To proceed in this direction it would be necessary both to tame the priorities and imper-atives of the political economy of private productivity and to redefine the counterideal of collectivity, which has inspired the left since the inception of capitalism.

Foucault's genealogies embody a critique of the ideal of self-con-sciousness or reflexivity that has governed critical thought in the mod-ern age. The pursuit of self-consciousness is the pursuit of a future in which all impulses that govern the self and all forces that govern the order are fully transparent to the participants. This ideal, crystallized most purely in the thought of Marx and Habermas, also finds more restrained expression in the thought of Hegel, Mill, and Freud. In its most optimistic formulations it is connected to radical understandings of community, legitimacy, and freedom. A legitimate society on this radical reading is one in which participants are conscious of its princi-ples of operation and freely internalize them as premises of their own conduct.

Foucault must see this ideal of self-consciousness and collectivity as the tyrannical twin of the liberal ideal of individuality. Reflexivity is a trap. It obligates us to bring the self more completely under the control of historically constructed standards of reason and morality; it draws us into confessional relationships in which therapeutic authorities first translate our dreams, wishes, and anxieties into clinical vocabularies and then hand them back to us as officially prescribed avenues to free-dom; and it sets the stage for political authorities to impose virtue on those who have not internalized the officially sanctioned standards of self-consciousness. "Western man has become the confessing animal," Foucault insists, and our ideals of freedom and self-consciousness func-tion to bring us more thoroughly within the orbit of normalization.

It is sometimes claimed against Foucault that his opposition to reflex-ivity at one level is contradicted by his contribution to it at another. Do not his genealogies make us more reflective about the ways in which the organized pursuit of self-consciousness functions to organize the self? Does he not endorse reflexivity in the act of opposing it? While this objection may be formally correct, the theorists who catch Foucault in this trap merrily return to those in which they themselves are caught; they remain untouched by new possibilities of reflection *they* acknowl-edge him to have opened. We can break out of this sterile circle of refutation and counterrefutation by *modifying* the ideal of reflexivity that has governed the left since the nineteenth century and by revising as well the ideas of legitimacy, freedom, and community to which it is linked.

By comparing the ambiguous orientations to madness and punishment in the late Middle Ages to the enclosures operative today, we can glimpse the elements of political conquest inscribed in contemporary practices. This is Foucault's contribution to reflexivity. And while we are immersed in the constructs and institutions that sustain these definitions, there is enough slippage, anomaly, and incoherence discernible inside them to support the suspicion that they mix together timeless standards of reason and defensive attempts to stabilize historically particular readings of the dualities of reason/unreason, self/other, virtue/vice, and normality/abnormality. One comes away from a Foucauldian encounter suspicious of the claim that these constructions represent universal truth and wary of any critique of them couched in the name of countertruths eventually susceptible to transparent formulation.

The modified idea of reflexivity suggested by these considerations does not pursue a future in which normalization, self-transparency, and freedom sustain one another. Reflexivity, rather, allows us to glimpse the limits of our own categories of classification and treatment and to confront, if obliquely, the defensive impulses that help to sustain them. We reflexively acknowledge that we lack sufficient resources to comprehend "the other" (those other people and aspects of our own conduct that escape established categories or transgress established standards). We acknowledge that there is much about the self that does and must elude us. If the Enlightenment struggled to dissolve the mysteries about the self and its world celebrated by traditional religious doctrines, the idea of reflexivity supported here brings us through genealogy to a secular appreciation of limits, antinomies, and mysteries lodged in the historical constructions through which social relations are organized. The point is to divorce secularism from the Enlightenment's hostility to mystery and ambiguity. Instead of treating deviations from established norms always as evidence against the deviants, we allow the persistent emergence of the other to bring us into touch with arbitrary elements in our own constructions. Instead of joining critiques of bourgeois or technocratic reason to a vision of a fully rational society, we allow genealogical deconstructions of past and present constructions to encourage us to oppose any future ideals of collectivity that promise to be governed purely by the light of reason. For the more fully we insist on standing in the light of pure reason, the more completely we are obliged to shove that which is out of place into the darkness.

Such an orientation does not entail rejection of all standards now available to us; for we could not live in any society if all standards were to be rejected. It does encourage us to adopt a more ironic stance toward standards we endorse, striving to detect arbitrary elements within necessary limits and to discern the shadow of injustice haunting existing norms of rationality. It also encourages us to project an ideal of order that can sustain itself without drawing so massively on the forces of punishment, incentive systems, therapy, self-containment, and civic virtue.

If the ideal of order suggested by these abstract statements acknowledges the need for limitation and constraint even while questioning the standards invoked to *identify* constraints and to *justify* the means of their protection, does it not deconstruct itself even before it has descended to earth from the heaven of theory? What *political* difference could be made by this appreciation of limits, ambiguity, and mystery?

We can consider these questions initially by recalling the tribal ritual practices mentioned earlier. Victor Turner in *The Ritual Process* has characterized these tribal rites of reversal:

> Each person plays and for the moment may experience the role
> of his opposite; the servile wife acts the domineering husband,
> and vice versa; the ravisher acts the ravished; the menial acts the
> master; the enemy acts the friend, the strictured youths act the
> rulers of the republic. . . . Each actor playfully takes the role of
> others in relation to his own usual self. Each may thereby learn
> to play his own routine roles afresh, surely with renewed under-
> standing, possibly with greater grace, perhaps with reciprocated
> love.[5]

One's initial reaction to these tribal rites is to paint a picture of an actual or possible mode of modernity in which they are superfluous, to insist that the elimination of established injustices is infinitely preferable to their consolidation through periodic rites of renewal. This reaction, though, mirrors the Enlightenment dream of complete rationality, justice, and transparency in social relations. It is as if *we* must pounce on the most obvious defect in the alien culture to ensure that *they* cannot help us to glimpse the madness in our dreams. I agree that it is imperative today to reduce inequalities of class and gender. However, once we acknowledge that the ideal of social life implicit in the demand to eliminate all limitation and darkness is a dangerous mystification, we must also suspect that our best efforts on these fronts will leave a residue of violence and resentment. Perhaps the extension of legal norms

5. Ithaca, N.Y.: Cornell University Press, 1969, pp. 185-86.

into new frontiers of social life both reduces the most blatant forms of injustice and diminishes the quality of those social relations newly absorbed into these forms. Perhaps the extension of litigiousness into new corners of life submerges one set of virtues while it realizes another.

The message for modernity within these tribal rites resides in the appreciation of the irony and ambiguity they embody. Acknowledgment of ambiguity within modernity tends to be reduced to a single-minded demand for justice. This devaluation of ambiguity in turn supports the denial, exclusion, and suppression of that which does not "fit" neatly within our norms and ideals. The rites express reflexively what reflexive impulses honed by the Enlightenment suppress: The norms and standards appropriate to the good life we prize together are also destructive in their impact on the other in oneself and other selves; the rites of reversal affirm this ambiguity and offer some degree of redress for the human losses incurred. The participants cannot articulate all the denials hidden in their affirmations because they swim in the culture which contains them; but they can set aside occasions in which the alien elements find some mode of expression by those who experience them most intensely.

Once we acknowledge that the technocratic ideal of reason and the radical ideal of collectivity share inflated conceptions of rationality, the unity of self, and social harmony, we can adopt an ironic stance toward norms worthy of endorsement.

Consider the treatment of the modern self as a subject. This self-identity, crucial to modern practices of freedom, knowledge, responsibility, and democracy, is a socially engendered organization that could have been (and has been) otherwise. But this acknowledgment does not require elimination of the formation. We may be particularly receptive, or at least receptive in important respects, to this form of identity. Since the human is incomplete without any socially established identity, there may be good reason to cherish this identity by comparison to previous and thinkable alternatives. And this appreciation may sustain itself even as we come to terms with ambiguities lodged in the self-identity of the subject.

We might come to see the subject as an essentially ambiguous achievement of modernity to be cherished while we modify our understanding and experience of it. It enables the democratization of social life (for the citizen is the subject at the level of politics); it provides an organization of self responsive to the human quest to examine the terms of our own existence. But the formation, imposed upon a being not predesigned to fit perfectly within it, inevitably spawns otherness in the self and in those other selves who deviate significantly from the standard it imposes. It is thus an ambiguous achievement.

To constitute the self as a subject, understood in some transcendental sense as the natural or true self, is to treat deviation from subjectivity as a lack, incapacity, or defect *itself* in need of correction or help. But to understand one's own subjectivity to be a partial and historical achievement imposed upon a being not predesigned to fit neatly into this mold is to understand that one's self-formation helps to create the otherness to which it reacts. To adopt this self-interpretation—this distinctive mode of self-consciousness—is to interrogate the relation between subjectivity and deviations from it in new ways; it is to question the single-minded interpretation of deviation as incapacity, defect, sickness, delinquency, irrationality itself in need of help. Such a formulation of self as subject heightens sensitivity to ways in which "help" given to others and to otherness flows first from the socially established need to fix the self's identity as a subject and second and problematically from internalization by the other of the need for this help.

Perhaps a modest example will illuminate this point. As social pressures to facilitate speed and suppleness in communication have intensified (pressures themselves worthy of explanation), those whose speech facility or reading comprehension does not mesh with this imperative become identified as victims who suffer from "stuttering" or "dyslexia." Former inconveniences now become "disabilities" or even "illnesses." We silently produce new disabilities and loudly debate whether their new victims should be helped to overcome them or penalized because they lack critical skills. But the defect here is not simply in the self: it is located in the form of life now requiring these skills to get along within it.

The best help we can give these parties, if we think about them alone, is to revise the rules of discourse so that such deviations from the standard become only modest inconveniences. Failing that, perhaps because it is concluded that the social good requires this speed and mode of communication, we can at least come to see that we have engendered the problem we seek to resolve and that redress is owed to those whose incapacities have been socially produced.

When the account appropriate to this modest example is applied to a larger array of phenemona such as sexual deviance, delinquency, "underground" economic activity, irrationality, irresponsibility, and retardation, they also assume a different appearance. We begin to ask how the tightening of social imperatives helps to create new abnormalities, deviations, incapacities, and delinquencies and how it might be possible to loosen or relax the circumstances that bring new forms of otherness into being.

The idea of the subject as an essentially ambiguous achievement of modernity is bound up, then, with appreciation of the need to rethink aspects of life that deviate from this standard, perhaps by seeking to enhance the social space in which difference can be without constituting a danger to the standard itself. The provision of institutional space for difference at once enhances the prospect for the subject to appreciate ambiguities in its own formation and encourages it to come to terms with the debt it owes to that in itself and other selves diverging from it.

But this space cannot be simply given as a permission. Such permission can always be rescinded, and those who receive it are constantly aware of their dependence on the sufferance of the donor. It must be established politically by actions that create what I called earlier greater "slack" in the institutional order itself.

An order that can afford to relax the reins of social control is one that can allow a rather broad range of behavior to *be,* only lightly touched by the pressure of normative standards. Where normative standards are essential, it still enables a large portion of negatively appraised conduct to be defined as odd, strange, eccentric, or wayward, finding it less necessary to convert so many of these negative judgments into operational concepts of illegality, delinquency, abnormality, irrationality, perversity, and obsolescence. The latter characterizations irresistably link judgment to institutional routines of decision, regulation, and control. They draw slack out of the order.

It will be said that the current American order provides considerable slack already, and that this condition (depending on the liberal or conservative stance from which the assertion is made) is already one of its greatest virtues or greatest vices. I agree that we are not stuck in a "one-dimensional society," but the United States is today marked by tendencies to rationalize and control broader areas of life, and these tendencies do not *merely* express the will of some to compel others to conform to their standards. The contemporary imperative to generate economic growth under adverse conditions of realization intensifies pressures to extend disciplinary control into new corners of life. If these imperatives are not met the order will stumble along dangerously, and if they are met it will be necessary to squeeze more slack out of the order.

In an order with slack the imperatives themselves are loosened. Because the imperatives are relaxed there is more room for us, first, to define our lives outside the medium of politics, second, for politics to serve as the medium through which we confront ambiguities within those limits.

Modern politics, at its best, embodies its own rites of reversal, but it cannot be at its best under current conditions.

This idea of slack, serving as a counterpoint to the logic of disciplinary control, itself stands in an ambiguous relation to radical and liberal doctrines. Echoes from an earlier liberalism reverberate within it. The classical liberal doctrine—in its support for constitutionalism, human rights, fallibilism, privacy, and the market as invisible coordinator of economic life—sought to protect the self from close dependence on state power and to restrict the space for political contestation. But while the doctrine of constitutionalism retains its importance, several other institutions and economic priorities in which liberalism placed its faith have become enlisted today as vehicles of disciplinary control.

The extension of private and public modes of disciplinary control flows to a great extent from the dual effort to foster economic expansion and to control elements inessential or disruptive to that course. Today slack in the order must be nourished by reconstituting the interdependent complexes of consumption, production, profit, economic growth, and resource dependence, which extend both underground evasions and disciplinary controls. The old liberal ideal of private space is now too tenuously connected to institutions and priorities historically defined by liberalism as essential to it.

The relation to established radical doctrine is similarly ambiguous. The position sketched here endorses much of the radical understanding of the sources of our economic condition while modifying the ideal of collectivity informing leftist opposition to capitalism. Once the contours of contemporary discipline have been delineated it is clear that a collective regime, not only through specific historic contingencies that block realization of its ideals, but also in its essential conception, contains the logic of disciplinary control. The collectivist ideal promises social unity and legitimacy through civic virtue; but while a measure of civic virtue is essential to a well-governed state, it is asked to bear far too much weight in collectivist ideals of life. It is not merely that the collectivist ideal implies unjustified confidence in the human capacity to achieve coordination through rational consensus, but also that it presupposes too close a harmony between the dictates of a well-ordered society and the character of the selves within it. Since the self is not "designed" to fit perfectly into any way of life, we must anticipate that every good way of life will both realize something in the self and encounter elements in the self resistant to its form; and we should thereby endorse the idea of slack as part of our conception of the good life. An order with slack can sustain itself well without the need to organize the self so completely into a creature of virtue. For the more an order needs virtue the more it eventually authorizes the extension of disciplinary strategies to secure it.

The experience of the twentieth century does not suggest that virtue should be expunged from politics, for a double dialectic of corruption and regimentation moves in to fill the gap opened by the disappearance of virtue. Virtue, though, is most likely to be sustained in a way of life that can flourish without having to extend the tentacles of order into so many corners of life. Slack in the order enables a broader range of behavior merely to be because the imperative to assimilate repugnant or eccentric conduct to the categories of irrationality or illegality has been relaxed. Slack at once reduces the space virture must cover and enhances the prospects for civic virtue within the space appropriate to it.

Slack in the order thus provides the antidote to those conscious and unconscious contrivances of social discipline emerging in the United States today to fill the gap created by the contraction of civic virtue and expansion of imperatives for social coordination. The key to its attainment surely resides in strategies to curtail the dual imperative for economic expansion and selective austerity that haunts the American political economy.[6]

Neither welfare liberalism nor radicalism today, taken in their dominant forms, speaks sensitively to the wish of citizens to participate in the common life while maintaining a degree of freedom from thorough entanglement in the forces of community and order. Each of these movements has lost touch with deep aspirations among constituencies it seeks to represent, and each now sees elements of its previous support drifting toward the right. Each must therefore cultivate new sensibilities to reestablish contact with its natural constituencies.

6. How could the twin imperatives of economic expansion and selective austerity be relaxed? My own guess—developed in Chaps. 2 and 3—is to revise the infrastructure of consumption so that the constant expansion of consumption *needs*, which fuels electoral pressures for constant economic growth and the imposition of austerity on marginal constituencies, could be curtailed. However, my point in this essay is less to consider how to foster these ends and more to argue that these are ends worthy of endorsement and exploration by liberals and radicals today.

8 THE MIRROR OF

AMERICA

The Dilemma of Epistemology

American analytic philosophy sustained itself for much of the twentieth century by ignoring the dilemma of epistemology enunciated by Hegel in 1807. Some analysts were confident that a valid theory of knowledge could be formulated; others were skeptical that this promise could be delivered. But most who addressed this problem assumed that progress in moral philosophy, social studies, and natural science depended essentially on the articulation of an epistemological foundation for these enterprises. All affirmed the primacy of epistemology.

The primacy of epistemology in American philosophy and social science manifests itself in the fetish of method, in the faith that the perfection of instruments of analysis (e.g., the rules of logic, test procedures, computer programs) will allow practitioners to squeeze truth out of their encounters with the world and to know that they have done so.

Hegel's account of the dilemma facing those who give primacy to epistemology has not, to my knowledge, been confronted directly by analytic practitioners. It can be stated briefly: every criterion of knowledge is itself a claim to knowledge and thus must itself be proven; but any attempt at validation must appeal either to the criterion itself or to a new criterion which is, in turn, in need of validation. The first strategy is circular while the second fosters an infinite regress. Each attempt to prove a theory of knowledge is doomed to disappear into one of these holes, and, as Nietzsche added, any new doctrine promising to establish an epistemic foundation will degenerate into either a tissue of self-deceits or a self-denying skepticism. The gloomy and pessimistic mood awaiting each new generation of defeated foundationalists constitutes an acknowledgment that the particular epistemology in which they had invested their hopes has failed and the continued insistence that social and cultural life must flounder until the epistemological dream has been fulfilled. The primacy of epistemology fosters the dilemma of epistemology, and evasion of the dilemma fosters passive nihilism.

Hegel, of course, became an indirect victim of his own prophecy, trying to transcend the dilemma of epistemology through an ontology susceptible of rational demonstration. His heroic failure was particularly illuminating. It revealed the depth of the dilemma and encouraged new generations of European intellectuals to avoid the embarrassment which, according to Hegel, plagued predecessors such as the "wise Scholasticus" and Kant.

> We ought, says Kant, to become acquainted with the instrument before we undertake the work for which it is to be employed; for if the instrument be insufficient, all our trouble will be spent in vain. . . . But the examination of knowledge can only be carried out by an act of knowledge. To examine this so-called instrument is the same as to know it. But to seek to know before we know is as absurd as the wise resolution of Scholasticus, not to venture into the water until he had learned to swim.[1]

Hegel's dilemma, thanks in no small measure to the recent work of Richard Rorty, must now be confronted by American analytic philosophers. Though he does not refer to Hegel's formulation, Rorty's own critique of "foundationalism" in contemporary American philosophy has a similar structure. Listen to his description of the enterprise to be dissected:

> "Analytic" philosophy is one more variant of Kantian philosophy. . . ; for analytic philosophy is still committed to the construction of a permanent, neutral framework for inquiry, and thus for all of culture. . . . It is the notion that human activity (and inquiry, the search for knowledge, in particular) takes place within a framework which can be isolated prior to the conclusion of inquiry—a set of presuppositions discoverable a priori—which links contemporary philosophy to the Descartes-Locke-Kant tradition. For the notion that there is such a framework only makes sense if we think of this framework as imposed by the nature of the knowing subject, by the nature of his faculties, or the nature of the medium within which he works.[2]

Rorty's deconstruction of foundationalism in contemporary American philosophy is powerful. His text, no doubt, will be subjected to the pincers movement which tried to move in two decades ago on Kuhn's *The Structure of Scientific Revolutions*. Practitioners on the right flank of

---

1. *The Logic of Hegel*, trans. William Wallace (Oxford: Oxford University Press, 1874), #10.
2. *Philosophy and the Mirror of Nature* (Princeton: Princeton University Press, 1979), p. 8.

the analytic establishment will dismiss the text by trying to show non-foundationalism to be self-refuting (forgetting to ask what effects the self-refuting character of their own foundationalism has on the power of this argument to discredit a critique of it), and a more liberal constellation will incorporate miscellaneous elements from Rorty's text into their own position while retaining methods and disciplinary priorities which presuppose foundationalism.

Rorty's achievement is fully comparable to Kuhn's in one respect, though not in another. For while Rorty effectively debunks the pretensions of foundationalism and the methodism it spawns, and while his account will foment disturbances in every corner of American philosophy, he falters in his attempt to chart an alternative course for theoretical discourse. Rorty closes the door he has opened just as the new converts are walking through it, and the pincers movement is likely to put the squeeze on nonfoundationalism unless that door is reopened.

Rorty's critique of foundationalism in American philosophy proceeds internally. Analytic philosophy, he contends, undermined its epistemic aspirations as it pursued the implications of its own premises. But most practitioners still struggle valiantly to evade the consequences. One group (led by Sellars) has dissolved the distinction between the necessary and the contingent—along with the transcendental arguments it authorizes—into the thesis that the "most fundamental postulates of rationality and epistemic authority" are "justified by society rather than by the character of the inner representations they express."[3] Another group (led by Quine) has dislodged the distinction between language as a system of reference and the facts recorded in it in deference to a holistic view in which linguistically mediated interpretation of nature and society is always possible but the appeal to a neutral set of facts against which to test a system of referents is not. When these two doctrines are endorsed, both the correspondence theory of truth, designed to show how a properly constructed theory mirrors the world it refers to, and transcendental arguments, designed to give universal stature to a self which constitutes the world in a particular way, can be shown to be relative to particular forms of social life. In combination these two doctrines transform foundationalism into a species of holism whereby each particular element within a theory can be checked to ascertain its rough coherence with the others, but no external test can be devised to test the truth of the system as a whole.

Unfortunately, most analytic philosophers cannot, Rorty admits, tolerate the results of these analyses. Acceptance of one of the doctrines is

3. Ibid., p. 178.

commonly balanced against precarious retention of the other. Analytic philosophy thus protects its methods in a new way. Its methods rest neither on securely established foundations nor on well-devised plans to break new ground in the future. Like the beams and timbers of an old barn, only the institutional matrix of analytic philosophy now holds the dilapidated structure together. Its representatives, for instance, now counter the work of Derrida, Foucault, Heidegger, Wittgenstein, and Nietzsche by insisting that they are not "doing philosophy."

Rorty's text is designed to help practitioners break out of this institutional matrix. When the rot in the old foundations is exposed, Rorty hopes, many will be prepared to build a new enterprise. "For the Quine-Sellars approach to epistemology, to say that truth and knowledge can only be judged by the standards of the inquirers of our own day, is not to say that human knowledge is less noble or more 'cut off from the world' than we had thought. It is merely to say that nothing counts as justification unless by reference to what we already accept, and that there is no way to get outside our beliefs and our language so as to find some test other than coherence."[4]

Rorty offers an interpretation of why the urge to epistemic foundationalism is so strong within the academic discipline of philosophy today. He calls it the "urge to philosophy" itself. For only if epistemic foundationalism remains credible will philosophy be recognized as the master discipline which assesses the methods and findings of the sciences, humanities, and social studies. The urge to foundationalism within philosophy is the wish to assume the cultural authority relinquished by religious authorities after the Enlightenment. Rorty, though more cautiously, further suggests that this urge is even more deeply rooted in our culture. As the secular embodiment of Nietzsche's "longest lie," it represents simultaneously one attempt to ward off doubt about the basic contours of our civilization and another to locate universal standards to validate the sense of injustice and alienation felt by many modern constituencies. The urge to discover foundations crystallizes into a doctrine within the discipline of philosophy, but it is also pervasively present in the culture at large. It is the continuation of religion by secular means.

Politics without Foundations

Various avenues lie open to Rorty after repudiation of the primacy of epistemology. Since he has drawn appreciatively upon

---

4. Ibid.

the work of Heidegger, Wittgenstein, and Nietzsche in making the case against foundations, one might expect him to follow some of them in charting an alternative course. But they are dismissed in favor of a pragmatism attributed to John Dewey.

Rorty's formal pronouncements, especially in *Philosophy and the Mirror of Nature,* appear to mesh with the hermeneutic doctrine associated with Heidegger and Gadamer in Europe and Charles Taylor in the United States. Thus when the point is to emphasize the contrast between foundationalism and "edification," Rorty dramatizes the exploratory, playful, engaged character of the latter enterprise. "The point of edifying philosophy is to keep the conversation going rather than to find the objective truth."[5] And while epistemic foundationalism "freezes culture," the edifying mode thaws it out, drawing us "out of our old selves by the power of strangeness, to aid us in becoming new beings."[6] We extend the conversation which constitutes us culturally by locating clearings within it and filling them in with new ideas, standards, and judgments; we change ourselves by pursuing uncharted possibilities within the discourse of our day.

But when Rorty, particularly in *The Consequences of Pragmatism,* actually participates in the ongoing conversation, he constantly wards off dangerous or disturbing possibilities within it. Rorty's language tranquillizes and comforts his fellow Americans, first, by celebrating the technocratic values, self-conceptions, and economic arrangements operative in (though not exhaustive of) American institutions and, second, by implying that once these endorsements have been offered there is not much more to be said. Rorty's prose inhibits discursive mobilization of political energies; it closes the conversation before it manages to disturb the sense that all is well with America. Consider a few examples (emphases added).

> It is simply that the pragmatist knows no better way to explain his position than to remind his interlocutor of the position they both are in, the contingent starting point they both share, the floating, ungrounded conversation of which they are both members. This means that the pragmatist cannot answer the question "What is so special about Europe?" save by saying, "Do you have anything non-European to suggest *which meets our European purposes better?*[7]

5. Ibid., p. 377.
6. Ibid.
7. *The Consequences of Pragmatism* (Minneapolis: University of Minnesota Press, 1982), p. 174.

In my view, we should be more willing than we are to celebrate bourgeois capitalist society as the best polity actualized so far, while *regretting* that it is *irrelevant* to most of the problems of most of the population of the planet.[8]

. . . pace [Charles] Taylor, it was a mistake to think of somebody's own account of his behavior as epistemically privileged. . . . But it is not a mistake to think of it as morally privileged. . . . Civility is not a method it is *simply* a virtue.[9]

Galileo and his followers discovered . . . that you can get much better predictions by thinking of things as masses of particles blindly bumping each other than by thinking of them as Aristotle thought of them. These discoveries are the basis of modern technological civilization. We can hardly be too *grateful* for them.[10]

And in the last paragraphs of his most recent text:

The split between two sorts of intellectuals has become deeper in our century. . . . It is the difference between the intellectual who believes that something like the "application of scientific method" is the best hope for human freedom and the intellectual who, with Foucault and Heidegger, sees this notion of "scientific method" as the mask behind which lurks the cruelty and despair of a nihilistic age. . . . One can call this a *political* split because both sides think of themselves . . . as the leaders who must articulate to their fellow citizens the dangers of their times. . . . Rather than pursue these issues, however, I merely want to suggest that we keep pragmatic tolerance going as long as we can. . . . In particular we should remind ourselves that although there are relations between academic politics and real politics, they are not tight enough to justify carrying the passions of the latter over into the former.[11] (emphasis in original)

Fundamental issues are posed in these statements only to be disposed of immediately. The considerations which guide Rorty's disposition of capitalism, the character of the modern self, the justification for listening to the self-interpretations of those who are objects of social inquiry or decision, the relation between technical control and the

8. Ibid., p. 210.
9. Ibid., p. 202.
10. Ibid., p. 191.
11. Ibid., p. 229.

The Mirror of America

quality of modern life, and the relation between philosophy and politics are barely audible. These just *are* his findings. His "regret" that capitalism is unable to deal with major world problems suggests that though this is unfortunate it is inevitable, and nothing can be done about it; when he calls capitalism "irrelevant" in its relations to the third world rather than, say, exploitative or inhibitive, he insinuates a mood of resignation into the text.

He says the decision to privilege the self-interpretation of participants in social inquiry is "simply" a virtue, implying that there is nothing to be said in favor of this judgment except that it is our judgment, and he happens to be one of us. How would he criticize those of us who disagree? When he insists that non-European ways are to be assessed by the extent to which they could meet "our European purposes better," he refuses to participate in a conversation which reconsiders those purposes themselves. Again, we are not told why he proceeds to this point and no further. He simply stops there. Similarly, we are advised to be "grateful" for the comforts of modern technology in a way which deflects attention from ambiguities, controls, and dangers residing in those achievements. And when finally the political dimension of the philosophical disputes examined throughout *The Consequences of Pragmatism* is noted at the end of the text, the issues constituting this polarity are buried beneath a pragmatic call to each side to extend tolerance to the other.

Rorty seems to think that after the demise of epistemic foundationalism he can "simply" let his conclusions do the talking, especially when they mirror technocratic dimensions of American society. It is as if he wanted to prove the foundationalist warning to be correct, namely: the demise of epistemology means the death of reflective discourse and judgment. Rorty is especially intriguing in that his assessment of technology, morality, capitalism, modernity, and the analytic style of philosophy (he compares it favorably to a lawyer's style) merges with the center of American philosophy even while he dismisses the epistemic basis provided for these conclusions, and his critique of foundationalism coalesces with those who join Nietzsche in exposing the longest lie of Western culture even while he then endorses the very technocratic values usually identified as the ultimate and most destructive result of that lie. But any enchantment with this anomalous stance, which at first seems to promise an extension of current horizons, is apt to diminish once it becomes clear how Rorty drops out of the conversation just when it should become more intense and demanding. What is left "just are" Rorty's "European values," his "ungrounded hopes," his "grateful" feelings. As one becomes progressively more attentive to the style which governs his writing, as one becomes more alert to its strategy of gaining assent, the Rorty philosophy of edification begins to look less like a hermeneutic circle which constantly calls its own preliminary judgments into question and more like a tinted mirror held up to American technocracy.

Phrases like "nothing counts as justification unless by reference to what we already accept" or claims that our most fundamental judgments are "justified by society rather than by the character of the inner representations they express" are ambiguous. They can signify either the primacy of hermeneutics over epistemology or the refusal to call the reigning values of one's own society into question. Rorty's formal pronouncements support the first reading even though his rhetorical strategies support the second. He thus trades one mirror for another; the void left by the demise of epistemic foundationalism is filled by a species of social foundationalism.

Dewey or Foucault

Can edification survive the death of epistemology, or does it flourish only while its opponent remains healthy? Is the philosophic urge essential to the quest to transcend the limits of the discursive world into which we have been thrown? The example of Rorty's political complacency supports the judgment of theorists like Habermas and Rawls who insist that the enterprise of social criticism requires some version of rationalist philosophy. But perhaps other avenues rejected prematurely by Rorty point in a different direction.

Consider Rorty's assessment of Foucault. In his reading, Dewey and Foucault share the same perspective. Each abandons the transcendental subject, truth as correspondence, and universal rationality. But Dewey, creatively consolidating judgments internal to Western society, projects a common life in which democracy and science flourish together. Foucault stifles this affirmative impulse, characterizing the same complex of institutions as a "disciplinary society," and he indicts the social sciences for their complicity in designing and implementing these disciplines. Rorty's characterization of the difference between these two nonfoundationalists is instructive. "Here we have two philosophers saying the same thing but putting a different spin on it." And again, "I do not think that we are going to find any *theoretical* differences which divide these two philosophers from each other."[12]

12. Ibid., p. 205.

The difference? Dewey offers "ungrounded hope" and Foucault a "pessimistic" indictment. We are left by Rorty to assume that when Foucault recovers from the shock of lost foundations he will realize that social life requires the harmonization of diverse impulses into common purposes and will reach the point at which Dewey has already arrived.

Something important is missing here, something beyond Rorty's failure to see that Foucault includes hermeneutics as an insidious partner of the conventional social sciences in helping to sustain disciplinary society. If Dewey and Foucault both repudiate the primacy of epistemology, there is still a theoretical debate between them, for *Foucault defends a non-Deweyan thesis in nonepistemic terms.* The thesis: there is no essence, telos, or purpose in the self which could be realized through a well-ordered society and hence no self-alienation in the existing order; but every order, by creating a self appropriate to it out of the raw material available, simultaneously organizes and subjugates the self. This goes for the plurality of selves within the individual in Homeric Greece, the moral self of the classical age, and the disciplinary self of modernity. In each of these orders there is always a resistant residue which does not mesh harmoniously with the self-constructions of its day.

Foucault adopts two complementary strategies, each of which is designed to support this thesis by indirection. At one level he strives to bring out the constructed character of the modern self by examining a series of radical shifts since the Renaissance in the relation between the self and the other. He uses the genealogies of madness, sexuality, criminality, and medicine to delineate historical shifts in the relation between reason and unreason and between self and other, revealing the historically variable character of reason and self. Both the constructed character of self and the deconstruction of a universal reason thick enough to establish one of these selves as authentic are revealed together. If the enterprise succeeds, we begin to experience ourselves as constructions. Thus, for example, Foucault's publication of *Herculin Barbin* allows us to listen to a being in the nineteenth century who did not fit into the gender categories of that age; we begin to appreciate the subjugation necessary to maintain the hegemony of universal gender duality. We are thus asked whether operative standards of normality permit the recognition and treatment of deviants, or conversely whether the social production of deviants maintains the power of arbitrary standards of normality.

The second strategy, most highly refined in *Discipline and Punish* and *The History of Sexuality,* consists of a rhetorical style which incites subjugated aspects of the self, evoking a response in readers which disturbs the artificial unity engendered through subjectification. Foucault's metaphors concentrate one's attention on the metaphorical character of a conventional discourse which pretends to be literal; by substituting "surveillance" for "observation," "interrogate" for "question," and so on, as described earlier, he incites a response stifled or cooled by the mellow metaphors conventionally used; and he challenges adherents of epistemology to prove how and why their soft metaphors carry more epistemic warrant than the trace of violence lodged in these alternatives. This series of rhetorical shifts is designed to speak to the subdued experience of disciplinary control, and *if* the self implicated in the discursive practices so characterized receives these messages, unorganized dimensions of the self may be awakened; the bearers of "subjugated knowledges" may be incited more actively to oppose established forms of control.

Foucault does not demonstrate the self to be an artificial construction or merely collect evidence which shows it to be so. He evokes the experience of constructedness while deconstructing standards which deny or delegitimize that experience. He does indeed draw us "out of our old selves by the power of strangeness" and perhaps "aid us in becoming new beings." He loosens the hold of "our" discourse and arguments by displacing metaphors which carry them, and we become more alert to the finely honed "discursive practices" within which our knowledge is "contained."

There may be, as I would argue there are, defects in the politics Foucault endorses and exaggerations in his decentering of the self. But he does not terminate the conversation once epistemology has been displaced; he extends it by encouraging us to experience strangeness in its prevailing form. A similar case could be made for Heidegger's exploration of the essence of technology as against Rorty's insistence that he arbitrarily introduces mystery where pragmatic acceptance will do well enough. Foucault and Heidegger replace epistemology with poetics, striving thereby to ventilate and illuminate the conventions which govern us. The internal discipline governing these texts allows us to interact creatively with them, and because each presents itself as more than the expression of mere feeling or opinion, we are able to question and criticize its governing themes.

Heidegger questions and illuminates; Foucault disturbs and incites; Rorty comforts and tranquilizes. Only one haunted by the ghost of epistemology would interpret these three thinkers to be "saying the *same* thing but putting a different spin on it." That assertion implies that only epistemic differences are *real* differences.

We can now assess Rorty's contribution to the conversation of American culture more precisely. He has launched a powerful attack on the

primacy of epistemology that exercises hegemony over American philosophy and social science, making it difficult for methodists to opt out
of the conversation about the foundations of epistemic foundationalism.
He has replaced foundational epistemology with a species of social
foundationalism which, though against his intentions, enhances our
appreciation of the critical impulses expressed in the philosophical urge
even while we draw back from the mystifications that urge seems to
require. And he inspires those impressed by this exposé of epistemology, and depressed by the aid and comfort it gives to technical
modes of control, to find ways to extend the conversation of our culture
in new directions. But the task, already begun in one way by Foucault
and in another by Heidegger, is still to show how it is *not* inevitable that
our "identification with our community . . . is heightened when we
take the community as *ours* rather than nature's, shaped rather than
found."[13]

13. Ibid., p. 166.

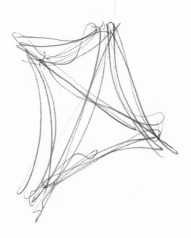

9   MODERN AUTHORITY

AND AMBIGUITY

The Issue of Authority

Authority is an indispensable and dangerous practice. Its dual character, present in every society, is particularly salient in modern societies. For the conventionalization of social life renders it more susceptible to imperatives of authoritative coordination and those subject to that coordination more resistant to its claims. Modern authority, at its best, is more respectful of individual dignity than previous forms. But any theory appreciative of this achievement must also attend to the burdens and dangers accompanying it.

Much of modern discourse about authority attempts to avoid its danger by defining one of its determining elements away. One constellation of theorists pretends that the dilemmas can be avoided by replacing (or at least supplanting) authority with coordination through incentive systems, making it in the private interests of persons and institutions to act in the public interest. But these theories conveniently ignore the authoritative background essential to the operation of such systems, and they also obscure the manipulative and coercive character of governance through incentive systems. Another constellation acknowledges the necessity of authority, but construes it to rest upon the consent of citizens who promise to abide by laws and rules established and enforced by proper procedures. Consent is in fact necessary to the modern practice of authority, but consent, when it is offered, applies not only to procedures for decision but to a larger set of understandings, ends, and purposes that help to constitute a way of life. Moreover, modern consent theories are too often articulated at a level too abstract to ascertain to what degree consent is spawned by coercive institutional pressures or offered within an institutional setting that enables it to be free. Consent theories are either too abstract to illuminate the modern practice of authority or too mired in the morass of issues occasioned by its dual character.

Another constellation of theorists would concur with the above points, but they interpret them to mean that modernity and authority must remain allergic to each other until the belief in a *telos* inscribed in

Modern Authority and Ambiguity

social life is restored to modern societies. Authority, from this point of view, is necessarily in decline because the basic ontological understandings of modernity are incompatible with its operation. There are important truths hidden in this latter formulation, but its basic premise and its stark conclusion are unfounded. *Telos,* in any strong sense of the word, cannot be restored to modernity, but the practice of modern authority is possible without such a restoration.

I wish to argue, first, that while the preconditions for traditional authority have receded, there is ontological space in modernity for a mode of authority appropriate to it; second, that this mode of authority is indispensable to a good way of life; third, that the most common substitutes offered to replace the practice of authority (i.e., interest manipulation and consensual morality) are, as full-blown *substitutes,* mad dreams which can become living nightmares; fourth, that the mode of authority appropriate to modernity involves an appreciation of its ambiguous character; and, fifth, than an appreciation of ambiguity must be installed in the institutional matrix of society if authority is to assume its appropriate place in modern life. I will not defend all of these claims with equal fervor, though each is part of the conception of authority I seek to explore.

Modern and Premodern Authority

Authority, according to Hannah Arendt in the first *Nomos* volume, devoted to this topic, can no longer be sustained in modern life because its ontological basis has disappeared. An external standard to which authorities can appeal has been lost.

> Historically we know of a variety of sources to which
> authoritative rulers could appeal in order to justify their power;
> it could be the law of nature, or the commands of God, or the
> Platonic ideas or ancient customs, or a great event in the past.
> . . . In all these cases legitimacy derives from something outside
> the range of human deeds . . .[1]

If we consider one of the periods when the ontological preconditions for the operation of Arendtian authority were secure, we might also delineate more clearly some of the distinctive characteristics of modern

---

1. "What Was Authority?" in Carl Friedrich, ed., *Nomos* (Cambridge: Harvard University Press, 1958), p. 82.

authority. The late Middle Ages combined several of the sources "outside the range of human deeds" in its theory and practice of authority.

Central to this world was God the Creator, the Designer, and the Sovereign whose will was discernible to humans, though darkly and imperfectly, in the things, events, words, deeds, and living beings that constituted the world. The natural world was alive with God's purpose; it contained a majestic harmony, a *telos*, which humans could glimpse if they exerted themselves in the right ways, and these glimpses gave them support and guidance in governing their lives. Authority, then, permeated this world. It could be found in sacred texts—a feature of the medieval quest for knowledge that encouraged it to look to the past to understand the correct order of things in the present. It was also located in spectacular events and in the fabric of those established customs and traditions touched by a divine hand.

Authorities, in this setting, claimed some privileged access to the purposiveness of the world. Through careful study of ancient texts or by living in communion with God or by being specially ordained by God, they could interpret authoritatively signs available to them and they could then act with authority. To feel the pull of authority in these circumstances is to seek to emulate conduct embodied in an exemplary individual or text. That is, perhaps, what Hannah Arendt meant when she said that "if authority is to be defined at all it must be in contradistinction to both coercive power and persuasion through arguments."[2]

The relation between a standard outside the scope of human deeds and human understanding of its implication for those deeds did remain problematic. Understanding of *telos* constantly faded into mystery and ambiguity because of the inherent limitations of the earthly commentators. But the signs were there to be read and they did provide a standard of appeal for authority beyond human deeds themselves.

A teleological ontology seems to presuppose a transcendental designer. Thus it is not surprising that the retreat of God from the mundane world, the withdrawal of telos from the world, and the decline of traditional authority moved together. We can understand why Hannah Arendt insists that religion, tradition, and authority engender one another, and moreover why the weakening of one element in this trio inevitably weakens the others.[3]

One way to characterize the shift from medieval to modern life at the ontological level is to say that subjectivity, previously finding perfect expression in God and imperfectly manifested in words, things,

2. Ibid., p. 86.
3. Ibid.

events, and living beings, now withdraws from its other spheres and migrates to the human self. The element of subjectivity (will and intelligent purpose) becomes concentrated in the self. And the world in which human subjects act is transformed by this migration. Nature, drained of telos, becomes either a set of unruly forces that must be subjected to human control or a deposit of objects to be understood through humanly constructed categories and used for human purposes; words no longer manifest divine meanings to be glimpsed by humans but are understood to be human constructions; knowledge shifts its locus from commentary on ancient texts to a grounding in human perception, experimentation, and logic. A whole new setting is thus provided for the definition and justification of authority, and it becomes questionable whether the ground of authority can any longer "derive from something outside the range of human deeds." Several features of this new setting deserve elaboration.

1. If subjectivity has become identified with the self, the self is thereby set up to be the standard of authority outside the scope of human deeds. The quest to justify authority in modernity is the quest to ground it in the rational consent of agents who agree (or promise) to obey rules and officials installed according to proper procedures. Consent theories face several difficulties—they pose the question of what characteristics of the self and what circumstances constitute consent, whether consent to a set of procedures can suffice to ground authority unless it is also linked to consent to a shared set of ends, and whether the new world possesses the resources to establish common ends worthy of consent. Two questions assume special importance. First, is the modern understanding of the self as an agent morally compatible with the exercise of authority at all? Second, is it possible to treat the subject as a transcendental standard against which a variety of historically lived understandings of the self can be measured, or is it necessary to see the subject as a specific product of modernity that cannot provide an independent ground for modern authority? Though the difficulties are severe, the relation among agency, consent, and authority must always be close in modernity; for without the element of consent the moral presumption of agents to accept authority can find no footing.

2. After the withdrawal of purpose from the world, after the corollary accentuation of human will and agency, social customs take on a new coloration. They become conventions that are, directly or indirectly, the product of individual and collective will. They are therefore understood to be revisable through willful action and to be hateful forms of constraint and imposition when they do not correspond to the will of those

living by them. When the conventionalization of social life is joined to the modern need to coordinate and organize so many aspects of life, the potential scope of authority broadens impressively. The disappearance of telos intensifies and extends imperatives of authoritative coordination by making each custom appear as a willful convention that could be otherwise, and it also weakens traditional supports for authoritative coordination. The tendency for those subjected to the will of authorities to experience that will as authoritarian is rooted in this interplay among the accentuation of will, conventionalization, and the intensified imperatives of social coordination.

3. The ontological background of traditional authority gives special place to the past in appraising performance in the present. This privilege is rooted for example in the epistemic status of sacred documents and in the significance accorded to founding acts in defining the propriety of current customs. The practice of traditional authority is inevitably linked to faith in the authenticity of those primordial moments; the authoritative character of those moments in turn is bound up with faith in the benign, if mysterious, intentions of a God who implanted signs of his will in the world. Faith does not disappear in the modern practice of authority; its basis and location merely shift. Modern conceptions of the world assume a more futuristic orientation whereby theories, experiments, and tests improve over time. And, similarly, modern projects are designed to realize an anticipated future more than to maintain or restore a pure condition located in the past. Thus the faith necessary to the operation of authority now becomes faith that obedience to a set of procedures, norms, and authorities today will help to foster the sort of world we want for ourselves or progeny tomorrow. Suspension of the wish to act on one's own wishes, interests, or judgments involves faith that the authoritative standards governing conduct today will tend in the long run to realize the ends that justify them. If the secularization of authority means that faith is translated into trust, it also installs the future as the connecting link between trust and authority. Modern authority is future oriented, and any understanding of its operation must contain an interpretation of the extent to which faith in the future our institutions are designed to build is justified.

4. If faith continues to be essential to modern authority, mystery does not disappear from its vicinity either. Rather it migrates from the relation between human deeds and cosmic purpose to the inner psychology of those over whom authority is exercised. The appearance of the self as subject, with its associated theory of consent, is haunted by the corollary appearance of theories of the unconscious and personal identification. These theories, murky and indefinite in character, seek to explain

why the pull of authority is sometimes stronger than rational considerations on its behalf, or why resentment against authority often seems to outstrip the onerous character of its demands, or why people sometimes pretend to accept authority when they are in fact subjected to coercive pressures. For instance, though the relationship between bidder and complier in any established relation of obedience typically embodies a mixture of authority, power, manipulation, and incentives, parties tend, when obedience is steady and secure, to inflate the importance of authority in the relationship.[4] The bidder, seeking to appear legitimate, can preserve that appearance by inflating the role of authority in sustaining obedience and deflating that of power; and the recipient, seeking to appear as a free agent acting on principle and not easily susceptible to coercion, is similarly encouraged to inflate the importance of the first element. Indirect signs enable one to interpret the degree to which such inflation occurs, for example when there is strict adherence to the letter of the law accompanied by creative efforts to evade its spirit, or when overt endorsement of the law is undermined by covert attempts to evade, elude, or subvert the application of the rules to oneself. The erosion of modern authority is much more likely to assume these latter forms than to find expression in the explicit repudiation of authority itself. If the ontology of modernity makes consent essential to the practice of authority, then these same circumstances also locate much of the mystery and danger of authority in the muddy waters of unconscious drives and personal identification. The enlightened, rational character of obedience through consent also locates irrational dimensions of authority in the depth psychology of the consenting adult.

5. A world drained of immanent purpose is one in which important human achievements are likely to be ambiguous. For if we are not designed to fit into a world itself designed to house us, then the designs we ourselves construct are likely to encounter resistance and opposition within the self and from the world. And any successful social construction is likely to require the exclusion, denial, or repudiation of that which does not fit within its frame. For example, the treatment of the

---

4. I explore the relation between authority and various forms of power in *The Terms of Political Discourse*, 2d ed. (Princeton: Princeton University Press, 1983). The relation between "in authority" and "an authority," which is presupposed in this essay, is also defended there. Richard Sennett's text *Authority* (New York: Alfred Knopf, 1980) includes a very thoughtful discussion of the psychological dimension of authority. The fear that the formal and justificatory side of authority may be swamped if its psychological dimension is emphasized is understandable. But the fear does not justify the tendency to ignore this dimension altogether.

self as a free, responsible subject also spawns delinquency, irresponsibility, perversity, and amorality as ways of being which fall below the threshold of responsible agency.[5] It is not that previous, less subject-centered forms of life lacked vice, but modern life constitutes otherness through the various ways in which it fails to live up to the standards of self as subject. The very constitution of subjectivity as a standard of selfhood encourages the formation and containment of that which deviates from the standard.

Similarly, if it is true, as it seems to be, that no way of life can sustain authority unless its members share a conception of the good life, it also seems true that any specific conception of the good life must exclude or denigrate elements that might otherwise be worthy of endorsement. They are excluded because they do not fit into the particular frame of good institutionally supported in that society. It is not just a fact, for instance, that extended kinship ties, along with the sociality and special supports they provide, do not flourish within a market economy. The fact is an index of the ambiguous character of any complex human achievement: it is possible, in a world no longer interpreted through teleological categories, to acknowledge that every complex social achievement contains unavoidable losses and that every established regularity tends to subjugate irregularities lodged within it.

When we understand nature to be an unruly set of forces not designed to coalesce with our needs, and when we understand the embodied self to contain elements that do not fit neatly into the social selves we design, we become suspicious of any social construct that appears to be fully harmonious or complete. The space for "deconstruction" and "genealogy" in modern life lies in the understanding that, since there is no ontological basis for the expectation of fully harmonious unities, each such apparent unity can be deconstructed—can be shown to contain anomalous, irregular, disparate elements that have had this unity imposed upon them. A theory of authority, indeed a theory of ethics or politics, that acknowledges this feature of modernity will also appreciate the ambiguous character of achievements it prizes the most.

We can crystallize the import of these five characteristics by saying that today consensual authority is fragile while alternative modes of social discipline possess self-regenerating capacities. Thus, the accentuation of will and convention, the expanded need for social coordina-

5. The most provocative treatment of this thesis is to be found in Michel Foucault, *Madness and Civilization* (New York: Random House, 1965), *Discipline and Punish* (New York: Pantheon, 1977), and *The History of Sexuality* (New York: Vintage Press, 1980).

tion, the orientation of the present to the future, the psychologization of authority, and the ambiguity of human achievements coalesce in some circumstances to render modern authority fragile. For the finely woven interdependence of modern life makes it relatively easy for disturbances at one point in the system to disrupt essential social transactions, converting what would have been a local disturbance in a previous age into a new trial of modern authority. The motive to disrupt the smooth operation of the system may flow from disaffection from the future it promises for oneself or one's children, or resentment against arbitrary treatment by authorities, or the sense that onerous conventions could be changed if only there were a public will to do so. The 1968 revolt in France, the Polish Solidarity movement, terrorist activities, and Teamster strikes and the Tylenol episode in the United States provide dramatic instances of the fragility of authority, while tax evasion, illegal aliens, public corruption, illicit drug dealing, and child abuse provide more insidious examples of the same phenomenon.

But some of the same elements that render authority fragile generate authoritarian modes of social control. For whenever a disruption is highly successful in unsettling established transactions, our very interdependency—the very lack of self-sufficiency in modern life—generates public consent (and sometimes urgent demands) to restore the smooth operation of the order by coercive means. Both the fragility of authority and the regenerative capacity of disciplinary control are grounded in the consent of the governed broadly construed.

This duality is built right into the structure of contemporary life. It is, one might say, one of the ways contrivances of social control (that is, the mix of authority, coercion, manipulation, and incentives discussed in Chapter 7 which regulate conduct in particular practices) maintain the appearance of authority when a more robust consent to its operation is not forthcoming.

The account given so far of the circumstances of modern authority has some affinities to Alasdair MacIntyre's *After Virtue*.[6] In modern life, MacIntyre says, where Aristotelian teleology has been "repudiated," virtue and authority tend to disappear. They are replaced by authoritarian, bureaucratic control and periodic eruptions of nihilistic violence. But MacIntyre's formulation is more stark than the one I endorse, and his remedy is at odds with the one I wish to pursue. For he contends that authority and virtue can be rescued only by restoring belief in teleology, and he thinks this is possible (if unlikely now to be

6. South Bend: University of Notre Dame Press, 1981.

adopted) once we correct defective understandings of self, morality, and society bequeathed to us by the Enlightenment.

Without developing the case in detail, I contend that strong teleological doctrines were not lost or repudiated; they rather came unraveled by the very attempts in the late medieval and early modern eras to perfect them. They exhausted and devalued themselves in the effort, for instance, to square the idea of an omnipotent creator with a world that limited God's creative will by expressing a rational design. Medieval nominalism sacrificed telos to save God; and the God saved became too distant from the world to maintain the supportive relation among religion, authority, and tradition identified by Arendt.[7] It is possible, after the self-destruction of strong teleological doctrines, to defend a much weaker version of the idea, in which telos, while drained form the cosmos, nature, and even to a significant degree from human bodies, is located in human projects. But the material deployed to realize those projects, because *it* can no longer be assumed to tend toward a natural harmony, also generates resistance and recalcitrance to their realization. A weakened teleology, when its implications are traced out, cannot sustain the traditional theory of virtue and authority MacIntyre advocates. It rather suggests an ethic of ambiguity. Any attempt to restore traditional authority and virtue in these circumstances eventually degenerates into an authoritarian effort to impose a unified image of the good on those who resist it.

Indeed, I suspect that the recent surge of interest in the Straussian distinction between the esoteric version of a doctrine and its exoteric presentation is rooted in the growing fear among theorists that authority and virtue, necessary to the operation of a good society, cannot be grounded without a strong teleology while the ontological basis for such a doctrine cannot now be established. Under these circumstances the exoteric formulation insists that the ground for the desired theory is solid, while the esoteric presentation acknowledges it to be very shaky indeed. The pretense of solidity, it is thought, must be sustained to ward off the nihilism that would result if the masses felt these rumblings beneath their feet.

7. The best account of how the self-devaluation of teleological theories emerged through the history of attempts to perfect the relation between God the Creator and the expressive character of the world is to be found in Hans Blumenberg, *The Legitimacy of the Modern Age* (Cambridge: MIT Press, 1983). His account reveals a series of severe defects in those theories which claim that we have unnecessarily repudiated or forgotten this legacy. It also, in my judgment, underestimates the difficulties and dilemmas internal to modernity itself.

Some theorists maintain the split between an esoteric doctrine reserved for a few prepared to receive it and an exoteric version offered to those unable to live with the truth; other theorists may contain the split within themselves, censoring internally thoughts and doubts that might prove dangerous if pressed very far. But wherever the split between the enunciated and the secret doctrine is located, it contains antidemocratic and authoritarian implications: the dangers such theorists court are more ominous that the ones from which we are to be protected. That at least is the operating assumption guiding this discussion of authority.

Authority and Ambiguity

What does it mean to acknowledge the ambiguous character of social achievements in the very practice of authority? Why is it a good thing to do? And what implications does it carry for the form of public life?

Consider first the case for affirming authority in modern life. It resides in the fact that every mode of social life selects from a broad range of possible ways of living together a smaller set that can be maintained within one social form. Order, then, implies limits, and modern orders additionally require extensive coordination of institutions and individuals to ensure that each meshes to a reasonable degree with the operation of the others. Authority, rightly instituted, is a mode of coordination that treats individuals with the respect due them without requiring each to possess an impossibly high degree of knowledge about every sector of social life or an unreasonably high level of civic virtue. It is an appropriate mode of coordination in societies where social knowledge is specialized, interests are diverse, and the requirements of common action are relatively high.

In circumstances where the ends served by the existing institutional structure are experienced as authoritative by participants, a preliminary condition is established for authority as one favored mode of social coordination.[8] But such an authoritative background, though essential to authority, does not suffice. Authority requires authorities who, because of the positions they hold and their mode of selection, interpret the specific meaning and import of that background in concrete set-

8. The connections and disconnections between the authoritative background and the exercise of authority are explored thoughtfully in Richard Flathman, *The Practice of Authority* (Chicago: University of Chicago Press, 1980).

tings. The open texture of the authoritative background, the need to decide between alternative interpretations of that background in specific settings to settle upon an authoritative rule, law, or policy, and the presumptive agreement by citizens to obey properly designated officials following prescribed procedures when social coordination is required coalesce to create the circumstances for authority, for the exercise of authority by authorities. In these circumstances there is a presumption in favor of obedience to authority even where many of those called upon to comply disagree with the decision or when it reflects beliefs from which they dissent. Authority is exercised over their specific actions rather than their specific beliefs (through its exercise still requires a background of generally shared beliefs).

When I voluntarily obey a traffic officer, a university dean, a union leader, or a judge exercising authority over me, I do so not merely because I agree with the necessity or wisdom of the verdict, or because I fear reprisal for refusing to comply, or because I want other people to make my decisions for me, but because I agree that the life we share in common requires commonalities of action in a variety of settings, that in some of those settings such commonalities are best achieved through authoritative coordination, and that this latter coordination, given the gap between particular imperatives of coordination and the porous texture of the common background of shared standards, requires authorities occupying particular positions to announce decisions, verdicts, and directives in their areas of competence. And this presumption in favor of the exercise of authority is supported by a background faith that over the long run its common acceptance will maintain and advance social purposes and ends we prize the most. When that faith disappears the operation of authority unravels; it gives way to disorder or to the other modes of social control or, more likely, to both together.

These considerations support a presumption in favor of the exercise of authority. But the ambiguous character of the authoritative background from which authority derives and the constant danger of its abuse support the case for an appreciation of ambiguity in the operation of authority. If there is no harmonious unity toward which individuals and societies tend, no state which, once reached, brings to unified fruition all of the ends and virtues worthy of our admiration, if we are accidents thrown into a world not designed to establish full harmony between nature and culture or between the public good and the good of the individual or within the self, we must expect that every operative set of authoritative norms contains arbitrary elements within it. These elements are not (or not necessarily) arbitrary in the sense that the preferred way of life could still be maintained if they were shucked off.

(They would then be eliminable evils.) They are arbitrary in the sense that, while they are indispensable to this way of life, there are other forms of living, admirable in their own way, in which this specific set would not be necessary. To see this is to see, first, that every good way of life imposes arbitrary limits, exclusions, losses, burdens, sacrifices on its members to sustain itself and, second, that these burdens are likely to be distributed asymmetrically across lines of gender, class, generation, or region.

To honor equality (an admirable thing) is also to demean excellence in certain ways; to institutionalize individualism is to sacrifice the solace and benefits of community; to exercise freedom is to experience the closure which accompanies choice among incompatible and often irreversible projects; to secure stable identities through gender demarcation is to exclude the hermaphrodite from such an identity and to suppress that in others which does not fit neatly into its frame; to prize the rule of law is to invite the extension of litigiousness into new corners of social life; to institutionalize respect for the responsible agent is to sow institutional disrespect for those unqualified or unwilling to exercise such responsibility; to give primacy to mathematicization in the social construction of knowledge is to denigrate individuals whose thought escapes that mold and to depreciate ways of knowing which do not fit into its frame. And lest the point be misread, to reverse these priorities would be to install another set of losses and impositions.

Any authoritative set of norms and standards is, at its best, an ambiguous achievement: it excludes and denigrates that which does not fit into its confines. Since social achievement is not possible without this shadow of ambiguity the question becomes: which achievements are worthy of our endorsement once the ambiguity within them is recognized? A second question also becomes pertinent: why is it that ideals which compete for hegemony today are typically articulated in ways that occlude the ambiguity residing within them?

It would perhaps be banal to iterate these points were they not closely associated with another. Nietzsche, who launched the most relentless assault on transcendental and teleological doctrines, also identified a powerful human urge to suppress disharmonies within our most cherished achievements. "German philosophy," Nietzsche says in *Will to Power*, pointing dramatically to its culmination in Kant and Hegel, "is the most fundamental form of romanticism and homesickness there has ever been." And, again, speaking of an urge found in every self, a longing which threatens to become an imperious demand, "one longs for that place in which one can be at home."⁹ When a child is homesick it cannot say no to the longing that overwhelms it; it demands elimination of the feeling of emptiness inside by returning to its home. The adult urge to find a home, to pretend that the best order to be realized in this world or another can resolve alienation, has fueled a series of ontologies in Western history that pretend to fulfill it. But we can now see through these pretenses and confront the urge propelling them. In doing so we support the case for authority while avoiding its worst dangers.

An established practice of authority is most dangerous when it expresses the urge to treat society as a home, because its exercise then functions to repress, exclude, deny that which is discordant with the harmony pursued.

The institutionalization of an ambiguous orientation to authority concedes a necessary role to authority while exposing dangers in the urge to integrate so much of the common life into its orbit. The most ominous danger confronting modern authority is that our experience of its fragility, in conjunction with the anxiety such experience evokes, will impel too many to concede too much to it, to suppress awareness of the dangers and injustices that accompany its successful exercise.

The institutionalization of ambiguity thus emerges as a strategy to confront and blunt homesickness within us. But how is ambiguity institutionalized? As I have said, some tribal societies contain rituals and myths that affirm the authority of the order available to them while acknowledging arbitrary elements in the forms through which they live. Thus the trickster myth, apparently finding expression in several tribal societies, evokes experience of disunities in the self and the world that cannot and should not find full expression in the common life. The Trickster, a protean self whose multiple centers of action conflict with one another, acknowledges a struggle others tend to suppress. Once when the Trickster was skinning a buffalo with his right arm,

> his left arm grabbed the buffalo. "Give that back to me, it is
> mine! Stop that or I will use my knife on you." So spoke the
> right arm. "I will cut you to pieces, that is what I will do to
> you," continued the right arm. . . . Again and again this was
> repeated. In this manner did Trickster make both his arms
> quarrel. That quarrel soon turned into a vicious fight and the left
> arm was badly cut up. "Oh, oh! Why did I do this? Why have I

9. Trans. Walter Kaufmann and R. J. Hollingdale (New York: Vintage Books, 1967), p. 225.

done this? I have made myself suffer!" The left arm was indeed bleeding profusely.[10]

The repetition of scenes like this in *The Trickster* evokes the idea that the organization of the self necessary to the good life shared with others is also destructive of elements in the self that do not fit into this organization. "The principle of ambivalence is incorporated into the myths and rituals of primitive peoples to an extraordinary degree. . . . And this laughing at oneself means accepting the ambivalence of the human condition, for which civilization gives us very little instruction or structured opportunity."[11]

There are other examples. The Lele, for instance, have a tightly demarcated set of categories for organizing the world around them. But they also confront limits in this organization by relating in a special way to things and animals that do not fit neatly into the categorical structure. To use Mary Douglas' terms again, they confront the dirt created by their own order through rituals of worship or pollution, acknowledging, though indirectly and obliquely, that the form they need to impose upon the world does not correspond to the world in all its complexity. Perhaps the most pertinent rites for our purposes are, as described earlier, seasonal festivals of reversal in some tribal societies where those normally in command are now commanded. These rites through their temporary character affirm the authoritative character of established norms, but through the mechanism of reversal they also provide a glimpse into the violence and sacrifices normally required to maintain it. When this ambiguity is ritually acknowledged, the normal way of life may be lived a little more loosely; more space may be sought for discrepancy and creativity within it.

These rites embody an appreciation of ambiguity, but they do so in a world morally and ontologically distant from modernity. The teleological conception of the cosmos within which the rituals are situated probably makes it easier to affirm ambiguities in the constructions of tribal life; for they can be interpreted as pointing obliquely to a higher order which is mysterious to humans but coherent and intelligible in itself. The modern appreciation of ambiguity cannot so easily rest upon this act of faith, and the resistance to its expression may thereby be more severe.

Modern ambiguity must find expression within a medium appropriate to its own structure of life. Politics provides the appropriate vehicle.

---

10. Paul Radin, *The Trickster: A Study in American Mythology* (New York: Schocken Books, 1972), p. 8.

11. Stanley Diamond, Introduction to *The Trickster*, pp. xii–xiii.

Modern politics, when the preconditions are right and it functions at its best, simultaneously operates to unsettle dimensions of the common life that have assumed a fixed character and to achieve a temporary settlement in areas where a common decision is needed but the resources of knowledge or administrative procedure are insufficient to resolve the issue. Modern politics, again at its best, is the institutionalization of ambiguity; it keeps alive that which might otherwise be killed by the weight of authority or necessity; it helps that which is subordinate to find its own voice and, perhaps, to expand the space in which it can be for itself rather than only for the order. If authority tends to concede too much to the yearning for harmony, politics encourages us to confront the urge itself.

Politics and authority stand in a relation of interdependence and opposition to one another. And this ambiguity, too, must be kept alive. For without authority politics degenerates into violence or coercion, but politics also provides an indispensable corrective to the intensification and overextension of authority. The forces in modernity that tend to displace politics, to convert it into administration or authoritative command or economic rationality or terrorism, subvert this appreciation of ambiguity. Indeed some of the same dimensions of contemporary life that render authority fragile squeeze the space within which politics can be the medium for the expression of ambiguity. This is particularly true when we consider the relation between modern authority and faith in the future available to modernity.

If faith in the future—in the future established institutions are designed to foster—is jeopardized, and if the established institutional structure is not easily or readily susceptible to redesign, the stage is set for the erosion of authority and ambiguity together. Something like that is happening in modern societies.

It is difficult to identify all the elements involved in this contemporary devaluation of the future available to our civilization. Certainly the capacity to launch nuclear holocaust is involved. Another source resides in the gap between the promises that legitimize the political economy of growth and the disciplines it must impose today to generate growth. Modern democracies depend upon constant economic growth to draw all citizens into the orbit of the good life they support and to temper the scale and intensity of social conflict. The institutions of work, investment, and consumption and the dependence of the state on tax dividends generated by the privately incorporated economy combine today to convert economic growth from an end into a system imperative. And the imperative is now pursued under unfavorable conditions of realization. Implicit doubts about the ability to sustain this pursuit into the

Modern Authority and Ambiguity

future and resentment against the disciplines imposed to fulfill the imperative encourage a variety of constituencies to evade and subvert the roles assigned to them. This proliferation of evasions in turn encourages state and private bureaucracies to devise more reliable means to maintain a closer connection between role assignment and performance. This dialectic tends to subvert authority and politics together.

Academic policy analyses defined around the problematics of "reindustrialization," "rationalization," "incentive systems," and "zerosum economics" all concede, though obliquely, that the disciplines required for the continued pursuit of growth must now be imposed on many who resist them. They implicitly acknowledge that faith in the future available to the civilization of productivity is waning and that authority and virtue must increasingly be supplanted by finely grained methods of social control.

Anyway, when confidence in the future recedes, authority gives way to other modes of social control, and these disciplines in turn accentuate impulses to resist and elude them. But, under these circumstances, each evasion, because of its destructive effects on system imperatives, eventually becomes the occasion for developing new instruments of discipline. Order is maintained, but authority, ambiguity, and politics tend to be squeezed. For the latter require a relatively high degree of confidence in the future established institutions are designed to realize and a reasonable degree of slack between the dominant ends supported by the system and the modes of conduct open to those who live within its confines.

The ontology of modern life is hospitable enough to authority and ambiguity, but the particular future contemporary institutions are designed to build may be rather inhospitable to both.

10 WHERE THE WORD

BREAKS OFF

The Mystery of Language

What is the relation of language to things, actions, practices, desires, and moods? And what are the implications for political discourse of these relations? There is, of course, a simple answer to this question. The words we use represent (or designate or picture) the things and moods which exist prior to them; a precise vocabulary will represent things perspicuously; and political discourse will be most perspicuous when it conforms to the canons of empirical science. This formulation obscures the mystery surrounding the relation of words and things, and it has already been subjected, in my judgment, to convincing rebuttal. But even when one is convinced of the insufficiency of the designative model, it is not perfectly clear how to remedy its defects. It is not that there are no alternative orientations available which purport to provide the remedy. There are at least three, which I shall call the constitutive, the expressive, and the genealogical, and while they converge in their objections to the designative model they diverge significantly amongst themselves on the lessons they carry for political discourse.

In an essay entitled "The Nature of Language," Heidegger draws our attention to a poem by Stefan George which ends:

> So I renounced and sadly see:
> where the word breaks off
> no thing may be.[1]

The poem asserts that words are essential to the being of things (and Heidegger says that "thing" is to be understood in the widest possible sense, covering anything which may be, such as a mood or a practice). The last two stanzas of this poem are preceded in Heidegger's text by a paragraph suggesting that the essence of language glimmers faintly for one when one strives to find the right word to say something and realizes that the readily available terms are inadequate. When this happens

---

1. *On the Way to Language*, trans. Peter Hertz (New York: Harper and Row, 1971), p. 60.

we are in position to ponder the complex relation between articulation and the world we seek to articulate, to ponder the meaning of the phrase "where the word breaks off no thing may be."

Consider the following sentences, each of which is easy to form in our world:

"She is an ironic thinker." (She makes assertions which call themselves into question and in so doing she asserts something about the character of the world or of thought.)

"Sentimentalism is a form of self-indulgence." (To feel nostalgia or grief is one thing, but when one focuses not on that which occasions these feelings but on the glory of the self who does the feeling, one detracts from the first-order feeling.)

"That is not boredom you feel but anxiety." (You express not, as you think, merely boredom in a particular setting, but a mood that contains a more pervasive and unacknowledged anxiousness about your life and its circumstances.)

"Mike, straighten up and pay attention." (The name "Mike" does not merely designate a person; it helps to individuate one; it enables one to be called into discourse. If our names were changed every decade or if each individual were nameless and only groups to which we belonged were given names, our conception of the self would be quite different. The self would not be a person as we understand that term today.)

The key words in the sentences above (ironic, sentimentalism, boredom, anxiety, Mike) do not merely designate that which exists independently of these formulations, nor does the articulation of these sentences itself simply constitute the states. Referential and constitutive theories of language do diverge importantly: one gives epistemic primacy to the thing described and the other to the subject who does the describing or to the intersubjective background of contrasts and comparisons which makes it possible for this state to be defined in the established universe of discourse. But both of these thematizations simplify the relation of articulation to that from which it proceeds. For articulation crystallizes or fixes in specific ways states which existed in inchoate form before they were brought into a particular web of contrasts and demarcations. Language is a loose web of meanings, each part of which helps to constitute others. In allowing any thing to be, it conceals that which does not fit into its frame. If the web were different the states would shift in character too; but were we not embodied selves in a world there would be no material from which articulation proceeds and no prediscursive element to return to in checking articulation for its adequacy or subtlety.

Several of the terms highlighted here are reflexive in character. A very simple universe of discourse would disable these articulations. In that world, these things could not be. One could be sad but not sentimental, for sentimentalism is an attitude toward one's own state of sadness. But in that world, too, the simple, brutish vocabulary would prove inadequate to human feelings inchoately experienced. Think perhaps of a group of children approaching their teens, dissatisfied with their childish vocabulary and disaffected from dimensions of the vocabulary into which their parents hope and expect them to grow. New formulations will be coined, and they will fix these inchoate states in ways which do not mesh perfectly either with their childish vocabulary or with the reflexive terms of irony and sentimentalism which govern the parents' world. To be in a transitional position where one experiences these alternative possibilities of articulation is to be able to experience the mystery of language and, perhaps, to glimpse its essence. Adult intellectuals seek ways to cultivate these transitional experiences artificially. For they are sources of both anxiety and creativity in our thinking.

The essence of language is glimpsed, Heidegger says, when we cannot find the right word. For those are times when we are in a position to see that "where the word breaks off, no thing may be." On those occasions one might experience the paradox of articulation: for things to be, they must be brought into a web of articulations which gives them boundaries, specificity, complexity; but any particular web of discourse fixes things in particular ways and closes out other possible modes of being. Moreover, neither "I" nor "we" are thoroughly in control of these articulations. My articulation is made possible by the fact that I move within a web of discourse which I can draw upon and extend creatively at its margins. And our broadest universe of discourse is bounded by our character as mortal, embodied selves who have a certain range of capacities for perception and reflection. Language, on this reading, is essentially poetic. It brings into being that which is available for articulation by a community of humans who speak, but it does so in particular ways, ways which express some possibilities residing within the material from which articulation proceeds by foreclosing others. We encounter (or glimpse) gaps in the discursive network whenever we experience—though of course this experience itself will be vague and contestable—the insufficiency of a particular formulation. For example, I feel the insufficiency of the terms within which contemporary discussion in America about the relation of words to things typically takes place. It seems to me that the official alternatives tend to be restricted to the designative and constitutive theories, and one is pressed to adopt the second theory if one finds imperfections or incoherencies in the first. But here, of course, there are subordinate traditions to draw upon to extend the range of possibilities beyond these two. Perhaps this is typically the case. A mode of discourse becomes entrenched, but it contains subordinate elements enabling us to extend its boundaries.

When we land upon a better formulation, when, that is, the idea of sentimentality or of the expressive dimension of language is introduced into a discourse which did not yet dramatize it, how, on the reading I have begun to give, are we to be confident that it is a better articulation rather than merely a new one? The designative theory teaches us to have recourse to the thing itself when this question arises. The constitutive theory offers two answers, corresponding to the individualist and communalist versions of the theory. The version which gives privilege to the individual as subject will try to provide a transcendental argument to show which categories are fundamental to the subject as self, and any viable articulation will have to fall within this frame. The version which gives greater privilege to the intersubjective background will validate individual formulations by checking how they cohere with the frame of common meanings available to a community. Both of these theories are subject centered, though they diverge as to the locus of subjectivity.

But if one decides that neither the designative nor the constitutive theory captures the complexity of language and articulation, neither of the corollary theories of redemption will suffice either: each simplifies the complex relation of words to things to enable it to identify a sufficient set of tests to resolve disputes between competing articulations. Indeed, it may turn out that the demand for redemption itself is somehow connected to the hegemony of these alternatives. At any rate I wish to think about this issue through elaboration of two alternative theories, neither of which fits within the designative or constitutive framework. Each of these orientations brings us, through its understanding of discourse, to a distinctive ontology of social life and then brings us, through its ontology, to a distinctive view of politics. These two orientations—I will call them the expressive and the genealogical—seem to me to join issues obscured in the previous debate. And each does so in a way that places it on a collision course with the other.

Expressivism and Attunement

Charles Taylor has provided an excellent account of the expressive theory in his recent collection of essays on language, politics, and ethics. His theory fits into neither the designative formula—which he criticizes extensively and effectively—nor the constitutive, though it might be said to contain designative and constitutive moments within it.

The expressive theory of language found its most robust expression in Western life during the medieval period and the Renaissance. In this world nature was seen to be alive with God's signature and purpose. By discerning resemblances in the world, say, affinities between the number of planets in the heavens and the number of orifices in the human body, we come to glimpse the purpose and will of the divine creator as they are inscribed in the world. To know in this setting is not to establish laws of nature experimentally. Knowledge assumes the form of commentary on meanings and affinities lodged in the text of the world. The world is read as a text. Authority resides within, or it is expressed through the words, things, events of the world. Dreams, madness, miracles, happenings reveal the text of the world to us, even while they conceal much of the purpose within it from us.

An expressive understanding of language emerges naturally in this context. Words reveal purposes, lessons, injunctions which lie in the will of Him who gave us the word, but, because of human sin and finitude, we can receive only a fragment of that will. The word reveals and instructs while it remains shrouded in mystery.

Now, Taylor accepts the repudiation of this view of the world which marks modernity while seeking to reconstitute an expressivist theory of language appropriate to this new setting. The old theory must therefore undergo significant modification. What is it, then, that language expresses in modern life? Well, first, it expresses feelings, moods, desires, aspirations which the self has only vaguely or inchoately before they are brought to articulation in a web of discourse. "If language serves to express/realize a new kind of awareness; then it may not only make possible a new awareness of things, and ability to describe them; but also new ways of feeling, of responding to things. If in expressing our thoughts about things we can come to new thoughts, then in expressing our feelings, we can come to have transformed feelings."[2]

One way of putting this is to say that the stirrings of the self are refined by being given definition in the intersubjective world of common meanings and contrasts located in the shared web of language which makes up a way of life. So, the subject (the self) is not the only privileged locus of expression here: the intersubjective web also contributes to it.

But Taylor sees that if the account stops here there is little critical lev-

2. "Language and Human Nature," *Philosophical Papers*, Vol. 1 (Cambridge: Cambridge University Press, 1985), p. 233.

erage to be brought to bear on the intersubjective setting in which articulation occurs. Some possibilities for revision and creative adjustment
will exist, for the experience of the self may not fit well with articulations
made available socially. But this is insufficient. Taylor seeks a telos of
expression which transcends the object (as in designative theories), the
self (as in theories which give primacy to the subject), and the intersubjective realm (as in theories which vest constitutive power in the community). The functional need for this space is clear enough. It would
provide an appeal that an articulation could make in defending its claim
to superiority over those already entrenched in the world it inhabits, a
superiority carrying moral and political implications within it.

Taylor introduces this aspiration in the form of a question posed in the
introduction to his *Philosophical Papers*. "Is what we are articulating," he
asks, "ultimately to be understood as our human response to our condition? Or is our articulation striving rather to be faithful to something
beyond us, not explicable simply in terms of human response?"[3] And
the direction of his own answer is indicated later when he compares
romantic theories of self-expression with another stance which incorporates and transcends them. "Some contemporaries would argue that
our most expressive creations, hence those where we are closest to
deploying our expressive power at the fullest, are not self-expressions;
that they have the power to move us because they manifest our expressive power itself and its relation to our world. In this kind of expression, we are responding to the way things are, rather than just exteri-
orizing our feelings."[4]

"We are responding to the way things are, rather than just exterioriz-
ing our feelings." Every one of Taylor's essays in the volumes under
discussion includes a statement moving the discussion in this way
through subjectivity to intersubjectivity and then through intersubjectivity to the larger world in which the self and the public world are
situated and to which they properly appeal. This is true of his discussions of freedom, personal identity, self-realization, legitimacy, and the
limits of epistemology, as well as of his discussions of language. I take
these statements to mean that discourse seeks to disclose a self-concep-
tion which harmonizes with our essential character as embodied selves,
that it seeks to project a social life in which the self is harmonized with
itself and integrated into a larger community, and that it seeks a corollary form of community in tune with "something beyond us." "We are
responding" means that expression is unavoidably a self-expression

3. Ibid., p. 11.
4. Ibid., p. 239.

that cannot mirror this world as it is in itself separate from our humanity; "responding to the way things are" means that we reach beyond the
self to its relation to a larger world and that we seek to become more
attuned to the bent in the self which harmonizes it best with that world.
Here one cannot speak of criteria which govern articulations; one can
speak only of articulations more or less attuned to the world and the
bent of the self. In Taylor's own formulation, "our attempts to formulate
what we hold most important must . . . strive to be faithful to something. But what they strive to be faithful to is not an independent object
with a fixed degree and manner of evidence, but rather a largely inar-
ticulate sense of what is of decisive importance."[5]

We can exemplify the model of articulation Taylor adopts by returning to the example of boredom introduced earlier. Suppose a friend
constantly announces that he is bored, that this announcement seems
both to reveal much about him (he is often restless, unable to find interesting things to do, etc.) and to conceal something more basic or fundamental about his condition. The articulation "boredom" fits nicely into a
subject-centered world where one is seen to be in charge of one's own
life, where activities and things are evaluated according to the extent to
which they are interesting to the self, where nature is experienced as a
depository of resources for human use and vistas to enhance human
pleasure. It probably had much less purchase as a term of self-dis-
closure in a world of multiple gods, a world alive with signs and injunctions, where danger to life was also a regular experience. To characterize
"boredom" as a paradigmatic mood of modern life is both to reveal
something about the character of a subject-centered world and to
enable a deeper or more resonant articulation of the mood itself.

Perhaps the persistence of this mood reveals how selves in a subject-
centered world, where I am supposed to be in charge of my microworld
and we are supposed to be in charge of the macroworld, become disturbed when they experience features of life outside their control.
Though a subject-centered discourse tends to ignore this fact, even subjects cannot eliminate their finitude. Death, the ultimate lack of control,
awaits each of us, and we tend to deflect attention from that necessity
by concentrating on the modest areas of life susceptible to self-control.
The articulation "boredom" seems to consolidate itself in a world where
we are supposed to be in control, where we often nonetheless feel
unease, and where death of the individual and the rising danger of
nuclear annihilation of the species provide dark counterpoints to this
myth. Boredom, when located in the broader matrix which surrounds

5. Ibid., p. 38.

and encourages its expression, also suggests the possibility of a more fundamental articulation that deepens and explains the first formulation without eliminating it altogether as wrong or false. Underlying persistent boredom is anxiety, a mood we are not encouraged to articulate in the subject-centered world, but which, once articulated, discloses or expresses something that had been obscurely present in the initial feeling. Anxiety is a vague malaise about the human condition itself, the new articulation may suggest, which is hidden when subjects are active, interested, involved, in charge of things, but which disturbs us vaguely and darkly when we step outside the hustle and bustle of everyday life . . . when we are bored, for instance.

The persistent mood of boredom is now reinterpreted: initially seen as a response to inactivity, it is now seen as an accompaniment to the injunction to be in control of one's fate by a creature incapable of shaping its fate in the most fundamental respects. The initial self-characterization helps to obscure the self-deception lurking in the subject-centered life of mastery and control. The rearticulation, claiming to reveal what had been concealed in the first reading, suggests the need for a more penetrating account of the intersubjective setting in which the idea of subjectivity receives its privileged status.

The expressive model, then, goes something like this. First there is a vague feeling that the self seeks to clarify, perhaps so it can be evaluated or eliminated or enhanced. Second there is a translation of the feeling into an established realm of discourse, a translation which defines it as a mood available for public appraisal and contrasts it to a variety of other moods also open to articulation in that setting. Next, there is a rearticulation which places the public realm itself under greater scrutiny, comparing the articulation readily available in this world to possibilities available in other ways of life. Finally, there is the claim that the new articulation is not just a different account, but one that deepens and corrects the first one. It brings one into closer attunement with one's own mood, and it draws one closer to a fundamental bent of the self. A variety of signs may convince one that such an advance has been made. For example, the new account may enable one to interpret one's particular sense of humor or even the cadence of one's voice in ways which mesh with this reading; they may now be seen to express darkly what the new articulation makes manifest. The quest is for an interpretation that is more self-revelatory and that points toward a way of life in which we are more attuned to the world we inhabit, including attunement to the self as an essentially embodied, finite being.

Taylor's account is creative in that it pierces through the limits of theories giving primacy to the object while it avoids the subjectivism (with its own set of paradoxes) which typically accompanies such a move. Taylor, it might be said, displaces the primacy of epistemology with the primacy of ontology. The rhetoric of articulation, attunement, expression, responsiveness, faithfulness, depth, and self-realization is designed to carry us through interpretation to a closer harmony with the world. But these terms insert a social ontology into discourse which itself might be interrogated. We are led to ask: does the pursuit of attunement draw us to an order in which we can be more at home in the world, or does it insinuate a fictional ideal into discourse which can be actualized only through containment of that which deviates from it?

These questions are politically relevant, for Taylor's quest for attunement inevitably loads his political priorities in a particular direction. He favors positive freedom over negative freedom, though giving space to the latter; he seeks to increase the possibility of self-identification with a larger way of life by increasing the extent to which it deserves allegiance; and he gives priority to the integration of otherness into a more rational community over a politics which seeks to give that which does not fit neatly into the order of things more room to be. In a recent exchange with me about the primacy of integration, he responded in a way which fairly represents his position on the other issues as well:

> Connolly's second question concerns the theory of personal identity. I can embrace as my own the one he offers to me, "in which the goal is to integrate otherness into more perfect forms of identification with the will of a rational community." This would seem to me the highest ideal. I have no idea a priori how far it is possible. Where it isn't, where differences are too great for people to coexist within truly self-governing communities, the second goal seems the appropriate one: "that we should strive to create more institutional space to allow otherness to be."[6]

Taylor himself is open to the possibility that the quest for community can "demand too high a price," but the bent of his theory consistently inclines it in the other direction. His theories of expressive articulation, of personal identity, of legitimacy, of freedom and, especially, of attunement all point toward an ideal of assimilation. The rhetoric of his texts consistently gives hegemony to integration, and from the vantage point of an ontology at odds with the quest for attunement, the articulations he sustains function to conceal or obscure the violence done to life when the ambiguous character of communal forms of identification is under-

6. Taylor, "Connolly, Foucault and Truth," *Political Theory* (August 1985), p. 134.

thematized. The points at issue here are difficult to articulate because they are lodged in the rhetorical configurations governing discourse as well as in the explicit arguments it sustains; moreover, they concern real effects on life that are not readily brought to a common court of appeal by parties who read these effects differently.

The best way to join these issues, I think, is to confront a philosophy of political discourse that endorses much of the expressivist critique of the designative and constitutive models while repudiating its philosophy of expressive attunement. Perhaps the comparison will show more closely how Taylor's intention to be open to "the price" life pays to the project of assimilating otherness does not synchronize well with the mode of discourse he practices.

The Genealogical Model

In discussing the genealogical view of language I do not mean to give an exhaustive account of genealogy per se. But the genealogical understanding of language and discourse serves, I believe, as an essential counterpoint to the expressive model. The appropriate relation between the two is the question I seek to pose. But first the model itself.

Genealogy treats unities and ideals typically construed to be expressive of nature, reason, human embodiment as such, or history as if they were social constructs subjugating elements within them recalcitrant to the unity established. It expresses, then, a view of history and an ontology at odds with those views which prop up rationalism and expressivism. It is the ontology it endorses, the relation it bears to language, and the means by which it establishes that ontology that will receive attention here.

Consider this statement by Nietzsche:

> In brief, the development of language and the development of consciousness . . . go hand in hand. . . . The emergence of our sense impressions into our consciousness, the ability to fix them and, as it were, exhibit them externally, increased proportionately with the need to communicate them to others by means of signs. The human being inventing signs is at the same time the human being who becomes ever more keenly conscious of himself. It was only as a social animal that man acquired self-consciousness—which he is still in the process of doing more and more.

My idea is, as you see, that consciousness doesn't really belong to man's individual existence but rather to his social or herd nature. . . . Consequently given the best will in the world to understand ourselves as individually as possible, "to know ourselves," each of us will always succeed in becoming conscious only of what is not individual but average. Our thoughts themselves are continually governed by the character of consciousness—by the "genius of the species" that commands it. . . . Fundamentally, all are incomparably personal, unique and infinitely individual; there is no doubt of that. But as soon as we translate them into consciousness *they no longer seem to be.*[7]

Notice the many points of intersection between this account and expressivism. First, both agree that an intersubjective (or herd) web is essential to articulation of moods, desires, perceptions, feelings. Second, both agree that the articulation does not represent a state which precedes it and is already formed, but clarifies, completes, and civilizes that which it draws into its web. Third, both agree that no complete account of unarticulated stirrings or sensory responses is possible; there is always material which escapes articulation even as articulation gives greater refinement, complexity, richness to the material it builds upon. Fourth, both agree that self-consciousness and articulation are intimately linked and that self-consciousness involves interpreting one's states and position in the world initially through the vocabulary of one's own world and then perhaps by reaching out to worlds (ways of life) quite distinct from one's own that help to throw implicit ingredients of that world into greater relief. Neither view of language in its relation to self and world could accept, then, the sufficiency of either a designative or a constitutive account of these relations.

These points of concord accentuate the fundamental difference between the two accounts. What genealogy cannot accept is the rhetoric governing expressivist texts; for that rhetoric insinuates a quest for attunement into articulation of moods, ideals, identities, identifications, and legitimacy which the genealogist must view as destructive and dangerous. To put the "claim" schematically (and I enclose "claim" in quotes to ward off the tendency to draw this metaphor immediately into the circle of epistemology): the rules of articulation do not mesh nicely with the logic of impulse, and the attempt to treat them as if they were concordant imposes upon the self even when it realizes something in the self.

7. *The Gay Science* (New York: Vintage Books, 1974), pp. 298–99.

When the unarticulated is folded into the web of articulation, that which does not fit "no longer seems to be," but it still works its effects. The task of genealogy, though it can be pursued only obliquely and indirectly, is to expose the falsification necessarily lodged inside articulations. It does not (cannot) counsel that one return to the pure state which articulation has falsified, nor can it come to know that which is falsified. It can, though, incite the experience of discrepancy between the prediscursive and the discursive in ways that teach us that cognitive articulations, while necessary and desirable, must not be allowed to exhaust life.

Questions immediately proliferate here. Why pay attention to that which escapes rational discourse? How, in any event, could I or we do so? What are the effects of such attentiveness, and, again, how could we "know" anything about these effects?

The expressivist seeks attunement to a world beyond the self which will somehow instruct us on the direction and form of the good life. He seeks to "remain faithful to" a higher unity or purpose to which conduct might conform. The expressivist, from the standpoint of the genealogist, yearns to discover a home in the world and projects this wish onto predispositions in the world itself. It is this dream which the genealogist must expose and uproot, for it contains the whisper of God's voice within it. That whisper is not audible to many, and we are wary of instruction from those who do hear it. From the standpoint of genealogy, expressivism is superior in one important respect to secular rationalism: it understands the imperative to locate the possibility of attunement in some space beyond the constitutive power of human subjectivity or intersubjectivity. It is, though, the quest for attunement itself that must be challenged.

In opposition to this quest for concordance with the world, the genealogist proceeds as if the world were truly indifferent to us and as if the human organization of experience never meshes fully with that which it categorizes and organizes. "World" here includes internal and external nature. "We must not imagine," Foucault urges, "that the world turns toward us a legible face which we would have only to decipher; the world is not the accomplice of our knowledge: there is no prediscursive providence which predisposes the world in our favor. We must conceive of discourse as a violence which we do to things, or at any rate as a practice which we impose upon them . . ."[8]

The genealogist treats the world and the body as if, since they were

---

8. "The Order of Discourse," in Robert Young, ed., *Untying the Text* (Boston: Routledge and Kegan Paul, 1981), p. 68.

not designed by some transcendent will, the points of affinity within and between them are partial and oblique, or, better, as if each affinity contains within it that which resists or subverts it. Genealogy seeks not attunement with higher unities, but attunement to discordance within the self, discordance between the self and the identities officially established for it, between personal identity and the dictates of social identification, between the vocabulary which encourages the pursuit of self-realization, identification, knowledge, and virtue and that which must be subdued to enable these formations. It is not (at least on the reading I endorse) that we can or should avoid articulating such unities, but we should seek to come to terms with that which is deflected, ignored, subordinated, excluded, or destroyed by these discursive formations.

There are at least four ways in which the genealogist loosens discursive strands woven around us. There is, first, a review of the urge within individuals and collectivities to construct such unities and to pretend that they are discoveries. There is, second, internal critiques of the history of arguments designed to establish teleological and rationalist theories, with the corollary suggestion that each new defeat calls the credibility of renewed attempts into question. There is, third, the presentation of strategic examples that clearly do not fit into established unities, compelling us either to find ways to draw these misfits into the fold or to acknowledge the element of dissonance or artificiality within the unities themselves. Finally, running through all of these tactics is an overt, openly deployed set of rhetorical devices that simultaneously expose the role such devices play in sustaining rationalist and expressivist orientations and incite the experience of discord or discrepancy between socially established unities and recalcitrant material within them. I will discuss further the last two strategies here.

If the designative theorist strives to describe the world as it is and the expressivist strives to draw us toward a way of life in which I am attuned to the form of life in which I reside and it is attuned to the larger world, the genealogist introduces secret, marginal, subordinated phenomena and discourses which, when exposed, disturb these plans and suggest that the previous obscurity of these phenomena sustained the appearance of neat representation or progress toward expressive attunement. An example is Michel Foucault's publication of *Herculin Barbin: Being the Recently Discovered Memoirs of a Nineteenth Century French Hermaphrodite*.[9] Alexina, the author of this autobiography, was first defined to be a female, then after a period of teenage difficulty, a male. Finally, this human whose body did not correspond well to either

9. Ed. Michel Foucault, trans. Richard McDougall (New York: Pantheon Books, 1980).

side of the male/female duality committed suicide. The autopsy used a vocabulary of male/female sexual organs to describe Alexina's anatomy.

> Is Alexina a woman? She has a vulva, labia majora, and feminine urethra, independent of the sort of imperforate which might be a monstrously developed clitoris. She has a vagina. True, it is very short and very narrow; but, after all, what is it if it is not a vagina? . . . Alexina has never menstruated; the whole outer part of her body is that of a man. . . . Her tastes, her inclinations, draw her toward women. . . . Finally, to sum up the matter, ovoid bodies and spermatic cords are found by touch in a divided scrotum. These are the real proofs of sex. We can now conclude and say: Alexina is a man, hermaphroditic no doubt, but with an obvious predominance of masculine sexual characteristics.[10]

A suicide followed by a medical representation of genital characteristics. But the report does not characterize the body neutrally: it insistently imposes first male and then female categories upon a body that escapes the duality governing the report. We insist that bodies fit into the duality we impose upon them and act as if we report actuality inscribed in nature. We then treat bodies that differ from these impositions as deviations from the telos of nature. We speak of defects, incapacities, deviations, imperfections, flaws in the body (rather then, say, in the social form that endorses this particular idealization of the body). Since our identities are bound up with clearly defined boundaries of gender, we must hide, alter, repair, help, or correct that which trangresses the boundary. But once we acknowledge the role imposition plays in fixing boundaries in these extreme cases, we begin to glimpse the more subdued role it plays in those more numerous cases where bodies deviate subtly from standards "nature" has set for them.

Today Alexina and numerous human bodies in analogous circumstances would undergo surgery to bring them into line with nature's intention. But no surgery could bring all of the anatomical, somatic, hormonal elements of such a body into neat coordination with this idealization. We are thus driven to impose the form socially as well as surgically upon bodies not designed to fit into it perfectly. In the twentieth century we also *say* (and we then seek to validate the saying surgically), "Alexina is a man."

If we were to modify the quest for attunement, perhaps the boundaries of gender duality might be loosened to let difference find a greater

10. Ibid., pp. 127–28.

diversity of expression. But that would require that we acknowledge and seek to articulate the elements of discordance in the unities we establish.

With such an example we can see how the genealogist might reinterpret the reading we heard the expressivist give to the mood of anxiety that periodically grips moderns. It is not merely that we moderns hesitate to thematize the issue of death. It is also that the official organization of self contains and defines as "other" elements in the self that resist or escape its imprint. Anxiety emerges, then, as the effect of a difference that must be defined and experienced as an incapacity or deviation, a difference that must therefore be subordinated or denied in the normalized self. The mood reveals, but the revelation breaks the mold prepared for it by the social ontology of expressivism.

The genealogist publicizes subordinate discourses and phenomena to loosen the hold that the most basic unities of our day exercise over official discourses. And this encourages a discourse which heightens the experience of dissonance within these unities themselves. Supporting and intensifying these genealogical arguments and exemplifications, then, is a set of rhetorical strategies designed to subvert the effects of the rhetorics governing analytical and expressivist texts. These strategies assume a variety of guises.

1. There is the displacement of unifying and ocular metaphors governing analytical and expressivist texts by more disruptive ones. When Foucault, for instance, speaks of the "insurrection of subjugated knowledges" or asserts that "the soul is the prison of the body" or calls panoptic observation "surveillance" or speaks of the modern subject as a real "fabrication," the point is to focus attention on an artificial and disciplinary dimension of these phenomena subdued by mainstream discourse and to suggest that the more mellow metaphors shaping the mood of mainstream texts constitute their textual politics even more than the logic of argumentation displayed there. The metaphors express the genealogical ontology of discordance within concord just as the expressivist metaphors carry their contrasting portrayal.

2. There is the conversion of noun forms giving the appearance of solidity to modern conceptions of truth, subject, rationality, gender identification, self-realization into terms that draw attention to processes which form and maintain them and suggest the presence of resistance inside these formations. Thus self-realization becomes normalization; the individual becomes the individualized self; and the standard of truth becomes thematized as the production of truth.

3. There is, as in sections of *The Genealogy of Morals* and *Thus Spoke Zarathustra*, the external dramatization of character types who can also

be read as voices jostling for a hearing within the self. This device, combined with metaphors that exaggerate and intensify subordinate voices as in a dream, enrages when it is read "literally," when it is read dogmatically as if these were the real monosyllabic positions of the author; but when interpreted as voices in the self it intensifies the experience of a plurality in the self that has been subordinated to a dominant stance. The monotonous formulations we ritually repeat are then experienced in closer relation to those alternative voices in the self which must be defeated or denied to spawn the self as a stolid metronome. The exaggerated statements, in these contexts, can be read as dramatizations designed to enable subdued voices (subjugated knowledges) to speak loudly enough to receive a hearing, and once the self is prepared to "listen to a different claim," those disparate elements from which modern subjectivity is crafted begin to be heard more distinctly.

4. There are minor stratagems such as the introduction of sentence fragments that do not conform to the conventional subject/verb/object form but communicate nonetheless, or the posing of innumerable "rhetorical" questions in the text which call attention to numerous areas of rational undecidability in contemporary thought and expose as well the willingness of contemporary thinkers to provide answers as if they were so decidable.

5. There is, finally, a mode of repetition in the genealogical text which exposes and counteracts the unconscious effects of repetition in mainstream texts. Advertisers and genealogists understand overtly the ways in which repetition fosters familiarity and familiarity induces tolerance or acceptance. The mode of repetition in a single genealogical text mimics and exaggerates that at work in the cumulative flow of mainstream texts, calling attention to underground agreements unthematized in intertextual politics and to the role repetition plays in establishing the acceptance of familiar formulations.

Genealogy, then, draws attention to its own stratagems; it enrages the rationalist who finds it to be manipulative, but it insists that manipulation finds more pervasive expression in texts where inverted versions of these strategies locate themselves below the threshold of overt attentiveness. There they do their work quietly betwixt and between the frame of rational argumentation. The question is whether the outraged rationalist objects more to strategies affirmed by the genealogist or to the embarrassment of discerning similar configurations secreted in the logic of rationalization.

"We must not imagine that the world . . . is . . . the accomplice of our knowledge; there is no prediscursive providence which predisposes the world in our favor." This is the message expressed through the rhet-

orical configurations and other modes of persuasion installed by genealogy. "We must not imagine" calls our attention to the central role our
own yearnings and imagination play in portraying the world as pre-
disposed to fulfill our most basic quest for fulfillment. The response to
such a yearning is not to disprove that which is not provable, to refute
that which is not subject to demonstration, but to expose the role imagination plays in these formulations and then to incite the experience of
discord in the self and its relation to the world so that this imagination
will be reconstituted. When the relation between our quest for a "home
in the world" and the projection of that wish onto the prediscursive
predisposition of the world is ruptured, we experience the danger and
destructiveness accompanying the pretense that the world is "pre-
disposed in our favor."

Genealogy simultaneously expresses a social ontology of dissonant
holism, confirms that the self finds completion only within a social
form, insists that every mode of completion—even though some may be
very superior to others—disables while it enables and defeats while it
realizes, incites the experience of discord within the self between the
social form it assumes and that subjugated by this formation, exposes
the subterranean role played by rhetorical configurations in supporting
more harmonious social ontologies, and prepares the self to support a
politics in which achievements are affirmed but the ambiguity within
them is acknowledged textually and institutionally.

Now, to emphasize the persistence of discrepancy between social
form and the selves and world drawn into it is not in itself to conclude
that every conceivable form of life subjugates equally, thereby making
moral judgment within and between such worlds impossible. Is this an
exaggeration imposed upon Foucauldian texts by opponents to enable
them to dispose of a difficult challenge? It certainly ignores the con-
tinuities he himself identifies within his famous discontinuities; and it
brushes off the stance of the fool he adopts toward modernity as incon-
sequential to the reading of the theory.

At any rate I wish to insist that the reading given here does not fall
into that dismissable category. The injunction is: do not imagine that
any social form does or could mesh neatly with the material from which
it is formed; do enhance moral sensibility of difference through genealogical devices that bring us to greater awareness of those multiple
points of discrepancy between institutional idealizations and that
which is contained or subjugated by them. Genealogy, or the reading
given to it here, is insufficient to political theory, but it is an indispensable voice in the chorus needed to make sense of our condition and to
establish agendas worthy of support. It is an adversary not of inter-

pretation or of political affirmation as such but of those modes of interpretation and affirmation that insist on treating the subject or the community or something beyond them as a unified ground of human being. Genealogy alerts us to voices of otherness subdued by expressivist and rationalist modes of discursive practice.

Poetics and Politics

But it will be said that this openness to the voice of otherness is surrounded by an enclosure. The injunction adopted here opens us to dissonance but forecloses prematurely the very possibility of establishing attunement with a prediscursive world "not explicable simply in terms of human response." Genealogy fixes the answers to the questions it poses.

The point must be conceded and reinterpreted. No text is open at once to all possibilities. Certainly the drive of expressivist texts gives priority to assimilation and attunement. When we acknowledge the impossibility of a neutral openness at this level of discourse, the case for a stance that counters the predisposition of rationalist, empiricist, expressive, and critical texts becomes much more powerful. In the context of contemporary discourse in America, the genealogical perspective enables us to establish some distance from underground assumptions shared by participants in the prevailing debates. Prejudgments they have treated as necessities now become possibilities that might be otherwise. Thought is freed from the tyranny of assumptions that seemed to be necessary because no alternative to them had been articulated.

My aspiration is to endorse a social ontology of discord within concord, to open discourse to voices subdued by the pursuit of harmony and identity, and to endorse a set of ends, principles, and standards worthy of admiration even when ambiguities within them have been acknowledged. One discursive test, then, of a standard or ideal is whether we can endorse it after ambiguities in it have been illuminated. The discussions of institutional slack, democracy, self, authority, and legitimacy launched in earlier essays in this text represent initial efforts to meet this test. I believe there are definite possibilities here, especially when it is understood, first, that we are essentially incomplete outside of social form and, second, that any particular mode of completion contains ambiguities within it.

We need the word, though not it alone, to give definition to social life, but the word also disciplines as it forms. Is politics, at its best, a medium through which to cultivate attentiveness to each side of this equation? Will attachment to difference in the world be enhanced if we imagine it to be a place where the word gives form to life; and where the word breaks off no form may be?

INDEX

INDEX

Aliens and unconscious controls, 101–2
Ambiguity: and authority, 127–28, 137–39; of democracy, 15–16; and dirt, 16, 94–96; of the good, xi, 133, 138; and loss of telos, 132; and modernity, 103–5; and politics, 16, 111–13, 140–41; and rites of reversal, 109–11; and slack, 96–97, 113–15; and the Trickster, 139–40; and the welfare state, 19–20, 79–81.
Anxiety, disclosure of, 149–52
Arendt, Hannah, 83–84, 128–29
Argument, self-refuting, 11–12, 55, 66. *See also* Genealogy; Rhetoric
Articulation and the unarticulated, 143–45
Attunement: and expression, 148–51; and genealogy, 154–55; and politics of assimilation, 149–51
Authority: and ambiguity, 127–28, 134, 137–39; the case for, 137–38; and contrivances of control, 132, 134; and discipline, 142; expressive view of, 128–31; and the future, 131; and politics, 140–41

Beautiful soul, 47–48, 83–86
Beauvoir, Simone de, xi
Bell, David, 74
Best, Michael, 39, 95
Blumenberg, Hans, 135
Boredom, and anxiety, 150
Burnham, Walter Dean, 31–34

Change, the dilemma of, 50–51
Citizenship and democracy, 3–4
Civic virtue: and self-consciousness, 62–63; and slack, 113–16
Common good: components of, 33–34, 43–46, 76–77; devaluation of, 31–36, 77–78; and intersubjectivity, 61–62
Community and individuality, 6–8
Confession and normalization, 108. *See also* Self-consciousness

Consumption: inclusive and exclusive, 29–30, 39–40; infrastructure of, 28–29, 77–78
Control: and authority, 132, 134; conscious modes of, 100; unconscious contrivances of, 99–103. *See also* Discipline
Convention: and authority, 130–31; and normalization, 4–6
Coordination, intensification of, 73, 99–101

Death and social identification, 42–43
Democracy: ambiguity of, 3–6, 15–16; and collective decision, 15–16; and Foucault, 14–15, 123–26; and Nietzsche, 14–15; and reindustrialization, 17–22; and self-formation, 15
Democratic Party: dilemma of, 37–38; reconstitution of, 38–41
Difference: attachment to, 160–61; as discordance, 9–13; and genealogy, 152–60; in the self, 14–16, 104–14; and slack, 112–15. *See also* Ambiguity; Dirt; Otherness
Dirt: and ambiguity, 16; as otherness, 11, 94–95
Disaffection: civic, 34–35; symptoms of, 34, 44, 69–70; and the welfare state, 79–81. *See also* Personal identity; Resentment
Discipline: conscious modes of, 22–25, 100, 132, 134; and democracy, 5–8, 17–22; and growth, 43–45; and humanism, 104; and power, 13–14; and productivity, 21–24; and reindustrialization, 21–26; and subjectivity, vii–x, 103–7; unconscious contrivances of, 99–103
Discordance: and genealogy, 153–55; ontology of, 9–16
Double: Foucault as, 92; Foucault on, 89–90

Index

COMPOSED BY LETTERGRAPHICS/CPC, INC.
KANSAS CITY, MISSOURI
MANUFACTURED BY INTER-COLLEGIATE PRESS, INC.
SHAWNEE MISSION, KANSAS
TEXT AND DISPLAY LINES ARE SET IN PALATINO

Library of Congress Cataloging-in-Publication Data
Connolly, William E.
Politics and ambiguity.
(Rhetoric of the human sciences)
Includes bibliographical references and index.
1. Political science.   2. Authority.   3. Ambiguity.
4. Legitimacy of governments.   I. Title.
JA74.C658   1987   320.2   86-15819
ISBN 0-299-10990-9